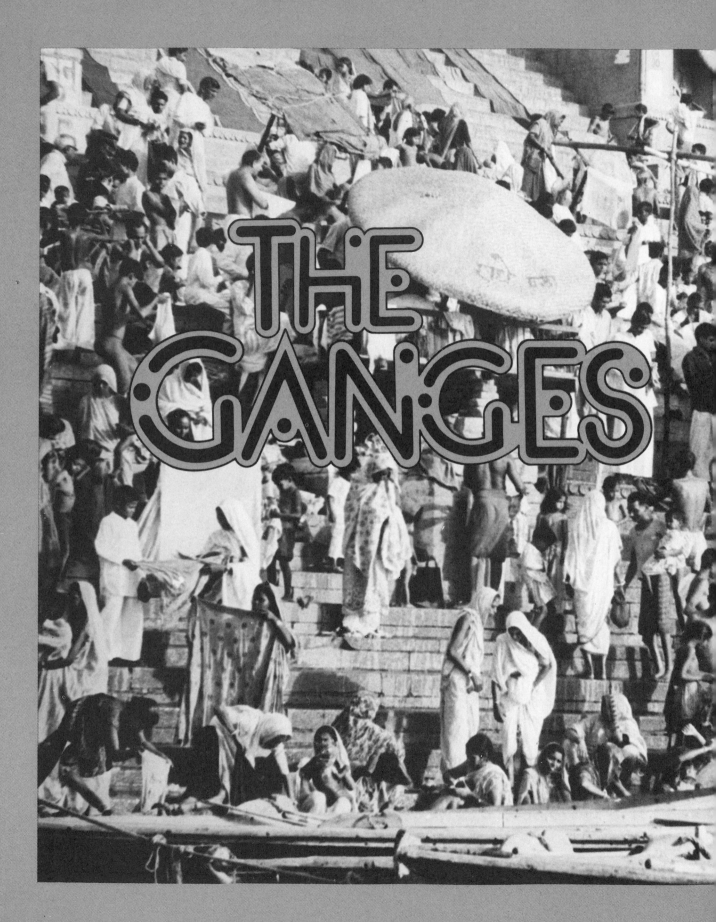

A Personal Encounter
by Edward Rice

photographs by the author

Four Winds Press
New York

Rice, Edward.
  The Ganges, a personal encounter.

  SUMMARY: Explores the history and course of the
Ganges, examining the land and cities along her banks
and her influence on the history and civilization of
India and Bangladesh.
  1. Ganges River—Juvenile literature. 2. Ganges
Valley—Description and travel—Juvenile literature.
3. India—History—Juvenile literature. [1. Ganges
River. 2. India—History] I. Title.
DS485.G25R5   915.4'1'03   73-88080

Published by Four Winds Press
A Division of Scholastic Magazines, Inc., New York, N.Y.
Copyright © 1974 by Edward Rice
Printed in the United States of America
Library of Congress Catalogue Card Number: 73-88080
1   2   3   4   5   78   77   76   75   74

CONTENTS

Map of
the Indian Subcontinent
& Gangetic Plain

AFGHANISTAN

Rawalpindi

Harappa

Lahore

PUNJAB

Saharanpur Rish

Hastinapura Hard

Delhi Meerut

New Delhi

PAKISTAN

Mohenjo-daro

GANGES UT

Agra

Ka

YUMNA

Karachi

Sagar

INDIA

Bombay

KRISHNA

Arabian Sea

Madras

Cuddalore

Cochin

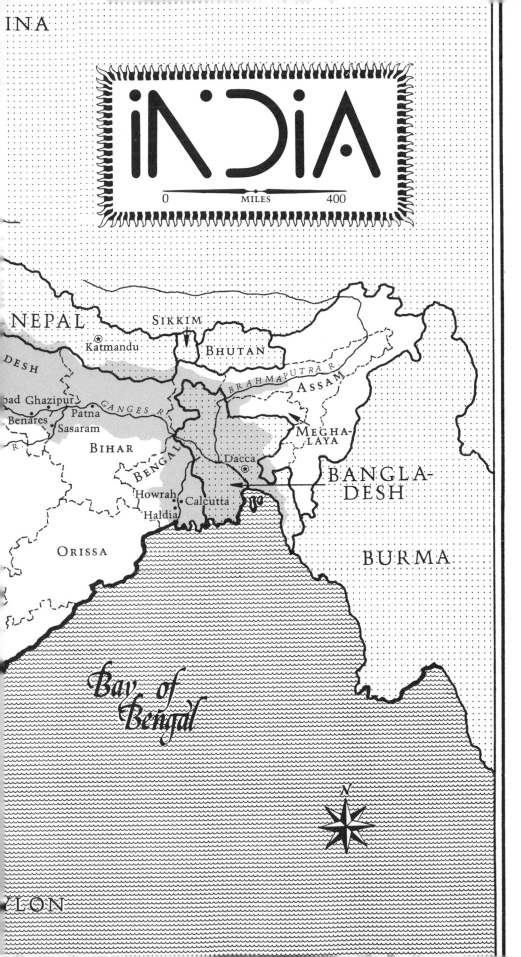

INA

iNDiA

0 — MILES — 400

NEPAL

SIKKIM

Katmandu

BHUTAN

DESH

BRAHMAPUTRA R.

ASSAM

bad Ghazipur

GANGES R.

Benares Patna

Sasaram

MEGHA-
LAYA

R.

BIHAR

BENGAL

Dacca

BANGLA-
DESH

Howrah Calcutta

Haldia

ORISSA

BURMA

Bay of
Bengal

N

*Shaded area indicates region
of plain of the Ganges River.

LON

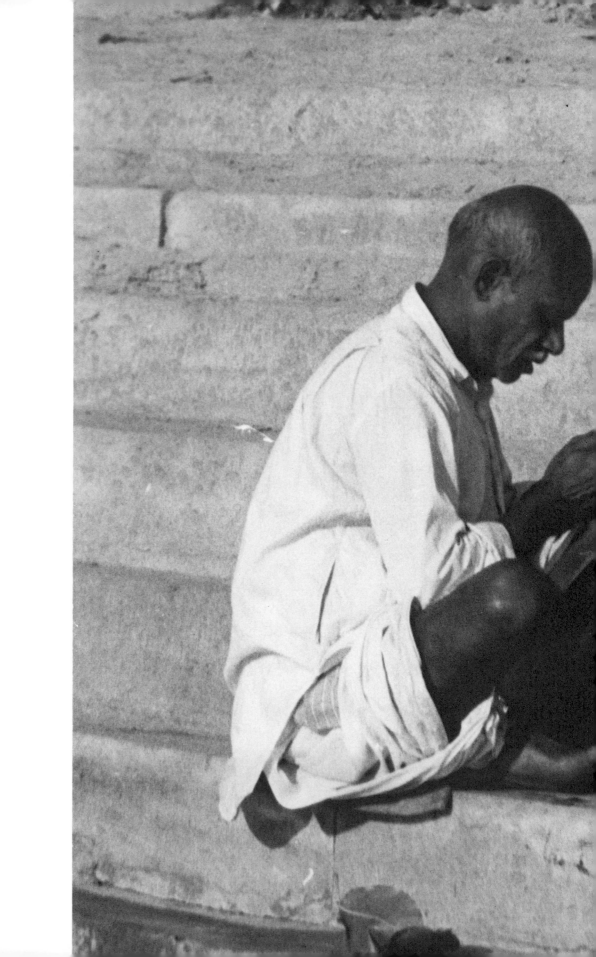

Gange Cha
Yamune Chaiva
Godavarai Saraswati
Narmade
Sindhu
Kaveri
Jale Asmin
Sannidhim Kuru

— The prayer to the Seven Sacred Rivers,
said by every devout Hindu while bathing:
O Holy Mother Ganges! O Yumna!
O Godavari! Saraswati! Narmada!
Sindhu! Cauvery! May each of you be
pleased to be manifested in these waters
in which I shall purify myself!

Foreword

The Ganges is the result of some five trips to India, starting with a brief visit to the Bombay and Cochin areas on the west coast. It was soon apparent that this great river is the heart of India, both ancient and contemporary. Therefore all of my subsequent trips involved long periods along the Ganges and her tributaries and in her great delta.

Though the river may make only a brief line on the map of northern India, some forty percent of the country's people live on the broad plain she has cut out over the aeons, and all of India draws more or less upon the river and the civilization she has nourished. Superficially the Ganges is just a big, slow-moving muddy stream, but if one is willing to sit upon her banks and meditate and try to absorb some of the "soul substance" that so many hundreds of millions of people have derived from her, it is usually apparent that the Ganges is more than a mere river. Her character comes not from her superficial aspects, but from her profound inner, sacred, mystical nature and from the people who live along her banks and pass their lives in devotion to her. It is a symbiotic relationship, river and people giving each other mystical sustenance.

I have written several other books with Indian themes. In each, as I probe deeper into the enigmatic nature of that continent and her inhabitants, I become more and more pried loose from my Western upbringing. I am thus likely to be more accepting of certain legends, myths, fables, stories about the Ganges than most Westerners. Consequently I present certain passages in a kind of "factual" tone which otherwise, for most Westerners, deserve some qualifying word or phrase, like "legendary," or "it is believed by Hindus." Why label the beliefs of another people or civilization as fanciful when our own world contains so many myths which we state in a matter-of-fact manner? Therefore I begin this book by saying that the Ganges is the only river in the world to drop from heaven upon the earth below. One can take this as fact, or myth, or poetry, in whatever way one wishes. The point is not to force our rationality upon other peoples' rationality.

E.R.

The Ganges

Rivers and mountains have a dual nature.
A river is but a form of water, yet it has a distinct body.
Mountains appear a motionless mass, yet their true form
  is not such,
We cannot know when looking at a lifeless shell that it contains
  a living being. Similarly, within the apparent inanimate rivers
  and mountains there dwells hidden a genie.
Rivers and mountains take the form they wish.

—From the Kalika Purana, a medieval work
dealing with the descent of the divine
to earth in the form of avatar.

History of Creation

The Ganges is the only river in the world that drops from heaven upon the earth below. Mother or Ma Ganga, as the river is called, falls upon the matted hair of the god, Lord Shiva, into a cave in the Himalayas, that formidable mountain range dividing India from Tibet and the great plateau of central Asia. The cave, which is the source of the Ganges, is almost three miles above sea level, and so remote that it is known more by legend than by the pilgrim.

On first sight the Ganges is hardly impressive. There are many rivers that are longer, broader, swifter. Certain rivers we rarely hear about, the Ob, Yenisey and Lena are all about twice as long as the Ganges, which runs a mere 1,514 miles. The Missouri-Mississippi, the longest river in the world, is 4,150 miles, and the other famous rivers are all much longer than the Ganges; the Nile being 3,600, the Congo 3,000, the Volga 2,400, the Amazon 3,505 and the Danube 1,725. On her upper reaches the Ganges seems like a mere trickle among a bed of fist-sized stones, the main flow being diverted into a parallel canal built by the English in the last century. Further downstream, on the great plain that is the heart of northern India, she flows silently, muddily, and so slowly that a leaf on her surface seems to be standing still. For most of her length the Ganges is a solid, earthy brown in color, the shade varying only in different lights or in different seasons, particularly in the monsoon floods, when she seems to be even muddier, having swept up hundreds of thousands of farms from her banks.

For the Hindu, Mother Ganges is a Supreme Being, a goddess. She bears an entire theology in her silent currents: not only is she an earthly river who lives and dies, fecundates and nourishes, but a heavenly one as well. The Ganges represents the "causal" waters, or ambhas in the Sanskrit, the waters beyond Heaven, supported by the sky. The ambhas are a product of the Universal Being, that is, Brahma the Creator. For the Hindu the causal waters are born of a long process of creation, springing from a desire of the god Brahma who first created the Fire that is Thought. In the Hindu cosmology, Fire wished, "May I be many and procreate," and thus the causal waters were born.

In a further development of the process of creation, the Water wished, "May I be many and procreate," and thus gave birth to food grains. Consequently, as man learned early in his existence, when the rains come from the skies and the rivers overflow and flood the parched farmlands, grains fructify and grow.

This elaborate history of creation, which may seem merely a poetic manner of phrasing a complicated process, takes on a different light in the harsh land that is India. Water, in a continent where the sun sears like a blowtorch and the earth moans and groans from want of rain,

Her farm swept away by the Ganges in full flood and her husband drowned, a desolate mother waits patiently in a shelter in East Bengal for aid. Too much, or too little, water means disaster for the Indian peasant.

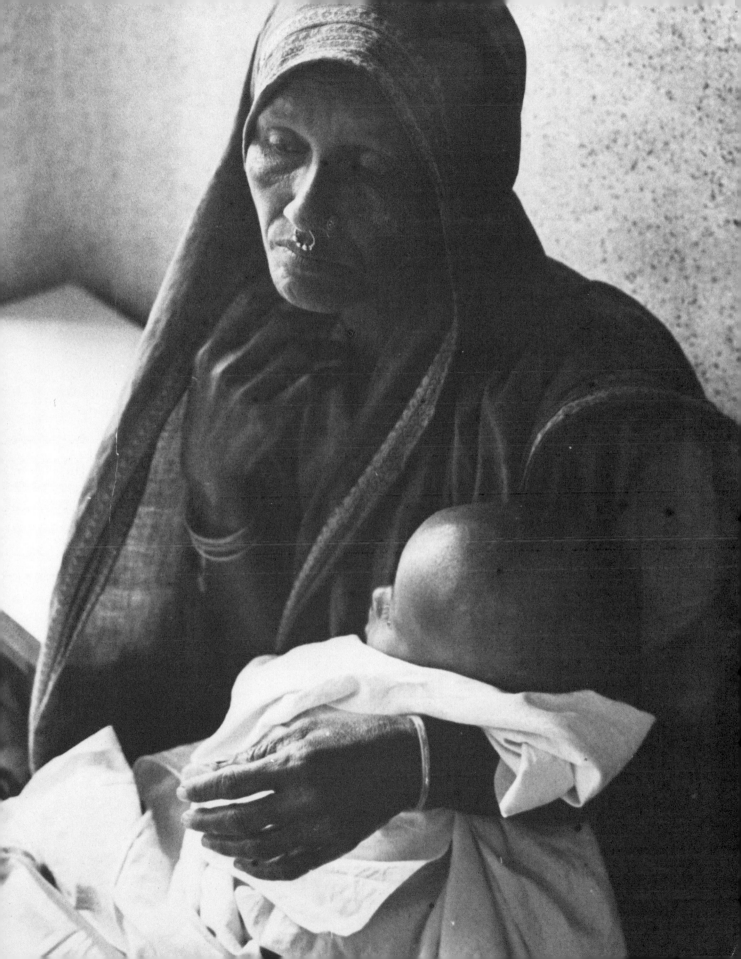

The god Vishnu, seen here in his multitudinous incarnations (they are reflected in mirrors), is believed to be the source of the Ganges in one legend. The river arises from his foot.

becomes sacred. Tumbling through mountain gorges worn deep in pine forests, then pacing herself in a swift torrent and finally as a great wide river moving patiently to the Bay of Bengal, Mother Ganges reveals herself in extremes, in terms of birth and death, creating and destroying, like the gods. The Westerner standing on her banks, ignorant of the passion Mother Ganges inspires, is at first inclined to wonder at the awe in which she is held. But eventually he feels himself growing, being absorbed into Mother Ganges. And in time, if he is at all receptive, he becomes a part of the river, as Hindus do, since in India all life, sentient and inert, is One.

The cave of ice that is the source of the Ganges is located in the Gangotri Glacier in the Garhwal Himalayas. Here it was, in some past time as shrouded in mist as the mountain peaks, that the Princess Ganga, daughter of King Himavat and the nymph Mena, was persuaded to descend to earth by the holy man Bhagiratha, a descendant of Sagar.

The situation was complicated in the manner that makes the ancient scriptures so hard to decipher. Sagar had been childless, a most distressing affliction in a land where children are so prized. With his wife Sumati, a young woman of unsurpassed beauty, Sagar performed the usual sacred austerities, and a sage named Brighu gave them the choice of having either one son or sixty thousand. Sumati chose the larger number and

A statue at Hardwar, one of India's most sacred cities, symbolically portrays the Ganges falling from heaven upon the god Shiva's matted hair. This is the common version of the river's origin.

eventually gave birth to a gourd, from which emerged her sons. They were carefully brought up by their nurses in jars full of *ghee*, a kind of clarified butterfat of great nourishment and sanctity.

After attaining manhood, the princes were sent by the raja to seek a sacred horse that had been meant for a ritual immolation, but had been stolen by a serpent god. The princes searched so vehemently that the universe was endangered by their energy. Eventually they located the horse, grazing nearby the sage Kapila, who, it seems, was none other than the god Vishnu in human form. In attempting to seize the sacred horse the princes angered Kapila, who cursed Sagar. With flames spurting from his body, Kapila reduced the raja's sixty thousand sons to ashes and sent them to hell.

The long, unexplained absence of the princes alarmed Sagar. He dispatched his grandson Ansumat to search for them. Ansumat found the heap of ashes, and as was the practice, sought water to perform the funeral rites according to custom. But his uncle, the god Garuda, informed him that it was not proper to use common water on this occasion. Only the goddess Ganga could perform the ceremonies with her sacred waters. Ansumat returned the horse to Sagar for the sacrifice, but the raja was unable to persuade Ganga to descend to earth to liberate his sons, even though he lived for another thirty thousand years.

Generations passed. Sagar's great-grandson Bhagiratha, at last through prayer and austerities, persuaded Ganga to descend from heaven "to wet the ashes of his ancestors so that they might then ascend to eternal heaven." The god Brahma, who had helped Bhagiratha, told him to ask the Lord Shiva to receive Ganga as she descended, as otherwise the earth could not sustain her fall. Bhagiratha then commanded Ganga to come down to earth. Angered at his abrupt order, Ganga assumed a form of amazing size and fell with tremendous force and rapidity, dropping abruptly upon Shiva's head, hoping to crush him with her weight. Shiva turned her loose upon the earth in seven rivers, the seventh of which is the one we call Ganga, or the Ganges.

But Ganga had not gone far when she intruded upon the sacrificial grounds of the sage Jahnu, normally a most holy and peaceful man. Angered by Ganga, Jahnu drank up all her waters. But the gods interceded, and the great Jahnu discharged Ganga from his ear. Now Bhagiratha mounted his chariot and led Ganga to the depths of hell, where she watered the ashes of the sixty thousand sons of Sagar, liberating them so they might return to heaven.

Flowing across India to the Bay of Bengal, Ganga purifies both celestial and terrestrial inhabitants, freeing sinners who bathe in her sacred waters. For, as the burnt sons of Sagar were liberated by her cooling depths, so will Ganga save all men.

The two great gods of the Hindu are Shiva and Vishnu, and most men follow one or the other, as Shaivites or Vaishnavites. The sects may sometimes dispute among themselves over which god assisted at Ganga's birth. Though Shaivites believe that to break her fall upon earth, Ganga flows through the god's matted hair; the Vaishnavites claim she rose from the big toe of their god's left foot. *Visnu-padabja-sambhuta* is the Sanskrit phrase in the litany of sacred names given the river. It means, simply, "Born of the lotus-like foot of Vishnu."

For mile after mile along the river, pilgrims enter the Ganges in prayer, hour after hour. The man wears the sacred thread of the Brahmin, the highest of the four castes.

We find that Mother Ganges is:

Melodious
Happy
White as milk
The milk-giver
Carrying away fear
Giver of delight to the eye
Eternally pure
Delightful
Resort of the eminent
Auspicious
A water-mine of nectar
Destroyer of sin
The creator of happiness
Perfect
The protector
Resembling the autumn moon
Peerless
Destroyer of sorrow
Bestower of happiness
Protector of the sick
and the suffering who seek refuge
Emancipator
Benefactor of the living

A light amid
the darkness of ignorance.

The river has 108 names, which form a prayer, recited by any devotee of her powers. I have given the simpler names of the *Gangastottara-sata-namavali,* as the litany is called, for many of the terms require an understanding of Hindu theology for full comprehension. Typical of some of the obscure phrases would be *Rna-traya-vimocini* and *Trigunatmika.* The first means "Releaser of the three debts," which is study of the Vedic scriptures for the holy man, sacrifice and worship for the priesthood, and having a son to carry on for the ordinary man. The *gunas* are "strands" which permeate every aspect of nature, and are *sattva, rajas* and *tamas.* Sattva, in simple language, is the concentration of energy. Likewise, rajas is the process through which creation in its endless variety of forms takes place in the divine mind. Rajas is balanced by tamas, the tendency towards dispersion, the dissolution into non-Being; it is liberation from all that binds.

The river "destroys the poison of illusion," she "brings about the continuance of peace," she is the "embodiment of the Supreme Spirit," and the "mother of what is alive."

The foreigner sees the river as a muddy stream, the land as an arid desert. Yet for the man who looks further, Mother Ganges flowing across India's parched plain is she who "Roams in Rose-apple-tree island."

Almost unseen in the burning sun and the sparkling waters, a team of coolies pulls their boat through the Ganges delta.

Geology

Two hundred million years ago the earth's land was one great mass, congregated somewhat south of the equatorial line. This single continent has been called Pangaea, or "all lands," by geophysicists. The continual inner churning of the earth, tortured by the heat of its molten-rock core, split Pangaea into two sections, Laurasia and Gondwara. The slow fracturing continued, and the continents gradually took the shape we know today.

The clearest example of the original fusion can be seen on a map of the western hemisphere and Africa: if one pushes the two together, it will be observed that the great northwest bulge of Africa fits into the upper half of the western hemisphere, while the bulge of the east coast of Latin America fits into Africa.

The flat chunk of land that we call India once was part of southern Pangaea, between the mass of the South Pole and Australia. The centrifugal force of the spinning earth drove "India" eastward across the uncharted ocean, freeing Australia at the same time. And then, roughly sixty-five million years ago, "India" rammed up against the southern shore of "Asia." The impact created huge ridges of land, several thousand miles long. These ridges—the Himalayan mountains—are higher than any other range in the world because part of India slipped beneath them, thus creating a double layer of land, tilting and raising a vast area so that a great plateau has been created some 13,000 feet above sea level. Mount Everest, the highest mountain in the world, is slightly over 29,000 feet, and some fifteen to twenty other peaks along the great ridges of South Asia are nearly as high. (Mount McKinley, the highest mountain in North America, is barely more than 20,000 feet.)

Thus the Himalayas sharply demarcate India from the rest of Asia, though the mountain barrier is by no means impenetrable. Traders, nomads, warrior tribes, migrating nations and refugees have always been able to find their way through the desolate mountains of the area (known today as Iran, Afghanistan and Tibet) into the steaming plains that are Pakistan and India. And merchant trade by sea has ranged all along the vast coasts since the dawn of history, making ancient India one of the most fabulously wealthy, exotic and magnetic lands known to man.

The mountains of the Himalayan range are vital to India because they are the source of the two great river systems which have watered all of northern India. In the west, the Indus and the five rivers of the Punjab (the name means Five Rivers) formed the heart of what may be the oldest civilization in the world. In the center and east, the Ganges with her tributaries (among them the very important Jumna, and the Sarasvati, Son and Brahmaputra) have formed the actual core of India, running through a great central plain on which Hindu (and then

High in the Himalayas a holy man sitting on the banks of Ma Ganga watches the sacred waters rushing toward the plain.

Buddhist and Muslim) civilization has been nurtured.

The Jumna and the Ganges drop down from the Himalayas in almost parallel lines, finally coming together after some 750 miles. The land between the Jumna and the Ganges is called the Doab (meaning Two Rivers), and has been the scene of great movements of people and ideas, of armies and ideologies. Here vast battles were fought ten and fifteen centuries before Christ, battles which are known today only in the form of legend and epic and in the culture and religion that developed from them. From the Doab's junction at Allahabad these great movements flowed eastward, across the dust of Bihar and the swamps of Bengal. In the not-too-distant past it was one of the most productive, fertile, creative lands of the entire world; at the time when western Europe was beginning to flourish in the glories of the Middle Ages, India was equal to anything the West could offer, and often surpassed it in wealth, productivity, creative talent and the level of ordinary life. Today, however, through overuse, deforestation, drought and overpopulation, India has declined until it ranks among the poorest nations of the earth.

In going eastward down the Ganges from the Doab, one senses a tragic decline in the quality of life, land and living. The land shrivels and dries, though the Ganges flows on imperturbably. Then as one reaches the Ganges delta, commonly called the Mouths of the Ganges, where the river is joined by the Brahmaputra which has come from Tibet

via Assam and Bangladesh, the Ganges breaks up into a number of rivers and streams. The most famous of these is the Hooghly, the river that serves the great port of Calcutta. Most of the delta lies within the tragic land of East Bengal, which after India was partitioned in 1947 was given to Pakistan. The delta is wet, steamy and interminably hot and humid.

On the central plain the heat reaches temperatures of 120°, but the air is dry, burning the moisture out of man, animals and soil impartially. In Bengal the air approaches 100 percent humidity and gives one the feeling of living in a bathtub. Indians suffer as much as foreigners. Indian friends tell me that though they have spent their entire lives in the delta, they are never fully acclimatized. While the heat and dampness enervates man and animal, they encourage the proliferation of their enemies, the minute bacteria, spores, fungi and nematodes of the soil, water and air that sap and destroy life, and spread disease and plagues which are still uncontrolled.

The mitigating factor of northern India, from West Pakistan and the Indus across the Gangetic plain to the Mouths of the Ganges in Bengal, is the monsoon. The rains come at slightly different times, but the late summer is the season for most of them, when they drop in great sheets, like lakes raised and then let loose upon the land below. They come endlessly, one feels, in spurts of a

Three slim women, baskets of fruit on their heads, cross a fragile bamboo bridge on a quiet backwater in the delta.

few minutes, or half an hour, an hour, for days. Since the land is flat, with the decline of the plain measured in inches per mile, excessive flooding is the result, and life stops, even in cities like Calcutta which exists literally on the water level. Then the sky, normally blank with heat, softens and colors and is filled with massive black clouds. The rains pervade everything. In the cities and villages the streets flood; on the farms the crops are submerged and drown. The land turns into a vast swamp. Mud houses collapse and the water licks away at the foundations of the stone temples; the plain is filled with whitewashed Shiva temples tilted like towers of Pisa.

In East Bengal the rivers rise above the marshy islands; people cling to trees or flee to Dacca, the capital, which offers some safety. When the rains end, the waters run deep into the thirsty earth; the skies are clear and turn a brilliant azure, the temperature falls to something almost bearable. It is now winter— November, December and January. (Most of India has but two seasons, unlike the West.) Now the farmers can plant and harvest. Crops grow quickly. By February the heat is returning, the land dries again and begins to crack. For most men, life becomes a question of rationing

As the river passes through Bengal, she breaks up into "mouths." North of Calcutta the Ganges becomes the Hooghly (below). Here, by a railway bridge, pilgrims bathe in the muddy waters. The land is so flat that flooding is frequent (left), even in cities like Calcutta, which is virtually immobilized during the rainy season.

Intertwined within the Indian soul are contradictory tendencies that reflect these extremes: the sensual pleasures and luxuries sought by the rajas, and the asceticism and self-denial of the yogis. This stark alternation, which offers no middle ground, produces in the man who has neither wealth nor the aptitude for saintliness, a grave dichotomy of soul and body . . . indecision, lassitude, hopelessness.

the harvest against the time when there is nothing but sun and heat and dust— day upon day, until the rains return. Some Indians think the stark extremes of too much sun on the one hand and too much rain on the other, with never a proper balance, account in part for the fatalistic attitude of the average man.

The Gangetic plain would not exist without the Himalayas. The two run almost parallel. Geologically, the Himalayas are a rather young range as far as other parts of the earth are concerned. Their great height is due to the fact that they have not had time to erode as fully as many older ranges. At their western limits, the Himalayas run into a series of other ranges that lead to the Atlantic. They form the southern border of the upland plateau of Tibet and lead into other chains of mountains that eventually border the Pacific. Not only have the mountains formed an effective barrier to large-scale penetration by humans, they also block off much of the fierce climate that sweeps down from the Arctic and are thus responsible for India's special climatic conditions, especially along the northern plain. These mountains, along with similar, lesser ranges, help form the type of weather known as "monsoon" and deftly place India within the area known as Monsoon Asia.

The plain now occupied by the Ganges was once a great tectonic trough, several thousand feet deep. It was caused by the impact of the floating mass of earth against the hard block of Asia. The collision of a vast mass of land against the solid and vaster mass of Asia produced a deep scar. Over the aeons immeasurable amounts of debris—rocks, plant and animal life, and particularly fine alluvial silt—have been brought down from the Himalayas by its rushing streams and rivers. These waterways, loaded with matter from the plateau and from the eroding sides of great gorges and mountain passes and rotting organic matter, fell into the Gangetic depression and deposited their accumulation of alluvium. Here it slowly piled up, and eventually, as the Ganges took shape and began to reach the form where it was able to flood the countryside, this alluvial matter was spread over the entire plain, forming a rich, fertile layer of soil. Well-watered by the river and her tributaries, this soil offered magnificent opportunities for the farmer.

India languishes in the fiery heat of the tropic latitudes, cooled only by periodic monsoons, and cut off from most of the frigid mass of Arctic air that covers northern Asia in the winter. Monsoon Asia extends from India's western neighbor, Pakistan, to southern China, southeast Asia, the Indies, the Philippines and the other offshore Pacific islands. The word monsoon is derived from the Arabic

A high-walled village reflects the prosperity that is often found in the Doab and on the plain among successful farming communities.

mausin, which means a seasonal wind. For the geographer, monsoon primarily denotes periodic changes in air flow, now dry, now wet, blowing in one direction part of the year, in the opposite at other times. But for the ordinary man in Monsoon Asia, who both profits and suffers under these climatic changes, monsoon means the heavy seasonal rains.

These climatic changes, unfortunately for the farmer whose crops are hopefully planned for monsoon rainfalls, rarely arrive at a fixed date with predictable amounts of wetness. The flows of air

over India that create the monsoon winds, wet or dry, are complicated and depend on weather elsewhere, but in general, some cooler air escaping over the mountain ranges strikes the steaming humid air of the Indian ocean, thus creating certain types of monsoon breezes which do not produce appreciable rainfall. At other times of the year, cool air sweeping around the eastern ends of the mountain ranges into the Pacific turns and flows south and westward to India, where it encounters low-pressure areas over the land. The result is monsoon rain, upon which the farmers of the Ganges and other areas rely for their crops.

The rainfall varies considerably. In the Ganges delta it reaches eighty inches or more. Upriver the rainfall may be only twenty inches, and further westward, in the desiccated Thar Desert that lies between the Ganges plain and the Indus plain there may be only five inches a year. In this area nature goes to extremes. In the low mountains of Assam, overlooking the Bengal delta, the locale of Cherrapunji averages some 450 inches of rain a year, and as the wettest place on earth even receives as much as 900

The great plain of the Ganges stretches for mile after mile. Centuries of dividing land among heirs have broken the farms into fragments. Here, two teams of oxen plough one small plot, while in the background another team works on another fragmented piece.

inches, while not far below, Bangladesh receives over eight feet of monsoon rain a year, most of it in the late summer.

The great plain that covers northern India and part of Pakistan is the largest of its type on earth, and has nourished a sizable number of people for close to 3,500 years. The rich alluvial soil supports a great variety of crops, of which rice and wheat are the leading ones. The plain itself, once covered with jungle, has been completely remade by man. Nomadic farmers and then settled peoples, rajas with estates, and Europeans with plantations have cleared away the original vegetation of great trees, vines, shrubs, ferns, flowers, roots and weeds, and driven off or killed the wild animals and birds that lived in the jungles.

On the western stretches of the Ganges, wheat is the favored crop. Here both rainfall and flooding are less, and wheat, along with other grains like millet, grows easily. As one travels eastward along the river, one finds that rice has taken over. It is the staple of much of India, and requires the extensive water of the lower Ganges and the intense light that is found on the Gangetic plain.

Rice farming demands a number of complicated steps, from germinating the grains on wet mats, to a series of transplants of the growing plants into the final planting in a few inches of water. The great flat sheets of wetland are known as paddy. The success of paddy depends on water, the river's or the monsoon's or both, and too much or too little, or ill-timed water, means the failure of the crop and a consequent

famine. If all goes well with the paddy, another kind of crop may follow the rice after harvesting as the earth loses its moisture, but has not reached the parched state.

The land has been farmed intensively over the centuries and consequently has lost some of its fertility, so the farmers try to observe a fallow period, usually every six years. One of the great problems is that the land has been fragmented by inheritance. Many farms may be no larger than an acre, and even these acres may be split, a piece here and there between the equally minute pieces of other men's farms. And as the population increases, the land is divided again and again. The equipment, too, is primitive. Few farmers can afford anything but the simplest types of plows, which are made

of wood. Digging may be done with a pointed stick. And many farmers are eternally in debt to local or town money-lenders. The problem of the man who loses his land to an absentee capitalist is constant, so that in many villages virtually all the farmers are landless yet are bound to the land to pay off debts and to support themselves and their families.

The rice crop is planted in the wet season in the late summer. If the rains fall on time and the floods are not disastrous, the rice will grow and mature and be ready for harvest in December and January. This is known as the *aghani* or winter harvest. The spring or *rabi* harvest, not always planted on the same land, produces some minor crops of bean-type legumes. Then come the *kharif* crops of the early summer, which may be corn (called maize in India), millet and some quick-growing rice for local consumption. In the eastern Ganges rice is grown as the food crop along with some tobacco, and jute, from which burlap is made, as the cash crop. Whatever the crop, the farmer's life is one of long hours and back-breaking work in the face of intense heat and unpredictable monsoon rains and Gangetic floods.

Failed rice crops stand sparse and dry in a drought-stricken paddy in Bihar. Weeks without rain have killed all growth.

*When the body is afflicted by old age
and disease, the holy water of Ma
Ganga is the medicine, and the Lord
Narayan [Vishnu], from whose lotus foot
Ganga springs, is the great
physician.*

— Attributed to
Lord Dhavantari, healer of the
gods, and through Vishnu's grace,
king of Benares, where he brought
medical science to earth.

Upstream
Rishikesh and Hardwar

The cave which is the source of the Ganges, if it exists is in the Himalayas, in Tibet, a forbidden land for virtually everyone, including Tibetans, since the time the theocratic kingdom was occupied by the Chinese. (I am told the cave does exist, but have not met anyone who has seen it, nor have I ever found a first-hand account of it.) Eventually the Ganges appears in a mountain torrent, dropping with a rush and a gasp of breath in mist and rainbows through cleft gorges. The mountains are steep and heavily wooded, full of wild animals and snakes. Hermits like to retire here among the natural caves to pass their lives in meditation. Pilgrims climb to these upper reaches, a difficult journey by foot, but there are no roads for motor vehicles. Pursuing Mother Ganges to her approximate source is a sacred rite. Ideally the pilgrim, leaving his home, walks up one bank and down the other. There are people who have made the complete trip from their villages to the source of the river and then down to the Bay of Bengal, where it empties, and back to their starting point. This, I suspect, takes a lifetime—worth it, one must admit, if salvation is the primary end of man's existence.

The Ganges falls past a few tiny, sacred villages, and at Rishikesh (the place of the *rishis* or seers), the breathless torrent is somewhat slowed. The river widens but the current is still powerful. Rishikesh is divided rather casually into two sections. On the eastern bank is a series of ashrams, or monasteries, and on the other, about a quarter or third of a

A nineteenth-century print shows sadhus at a site in Rishikesh. They are painted

with various symbols indicating that they follow Lord Shiva.

mile to the south, is a jumble of undistinguished buildings looking as if no one had had the time or energy to complete them. The road up to Rishikesh from the plain brings one first into the town. To reach the ashrams, one takes the pilgrim ferry, which wanders back and forth casually from one bank to another packed to overflowing with yogis, sadhus, swamis, sannyasis, Vaishnavites and Shaivites, and other holy people, pilgrims and tourists. From time to time the boats are so packed they threaten to dump the entire crowd into the river. Accidents have happened, but for most people this is as sure a means of gaining salvation as any.

Rishikesh is the first important town on the Ganges as she flows southward and is one of the Seven Sacred Cities and a famous pilgrim center, along with Hardwar, her companion town fifteen miles below. This is what is called a "prohibited area" for food—meat, eggs and fish are forbidden. Most Hindus are vegetarians; only the most "enlightened" or those without caste will touch meat; a larger number of Hindus eat eggs and fish, but in Rishikesh and Hardwar no Hindu of any sect would violate the ancient proscriptions.

There is a tiny sandy beach on either bank, but it is peppered with smoothly worn stones about the size of tangerines and lots of heavy, chunky boulders. Holy men often sit by the hour on the boulders in meditation, their backs stiff and their hands in their laps, their legs folded in the lotus position. Many of the holy men are attached to ashrams. At Rishikesh

the ashrams seem to run into each other along the eastern bank; they are jammed together as if there was no other space in all of India, but each is a unity representing a different sect or founder, or a different method of contemplation. Some are built of white stone or are painted white, others are a deep red, some are simple and austere, others a florid combination of gardens, shops, statues, banners, signs and meditation rooms, accented by loudspeakers which repeat endless religious hymns that sound more like Indian movie music than chants from the Vedas and other ancient scriptures.

Going south along the western shore the beach widens; there is more fine white sand, and more stones and boulders. Hermits sit silently everywhere, absorbed by the river. Most Westerners come to see the Mahesh Yogi, otherwise known as the Maharishi. Indians who pay attention to foreigners are likely to call out "Beatles' Yogi" and point toward a road leading up a hill to the forest that conceals the complex of buildings of his ashram. The Maharishi has an ineffable attraction for the Westerner. I had heard him in New York, and was not impressed, but here, on the sandy shore of the Ganges, I felt a pull and finally decided not to resist. The road to his ashram winds through a heavy forest; one comes to a clearing with a new, tall cast-cement building which looks like a miniature Hilton. This is the guest house for the Yogi's disciples, who are invariably Westerners; Indians, in my experience, think that his commercialism makes him either a joke or a fraud and will have nothing to do with him.

Beyond the guest house are a number of smaller buildings, one a large rambling bungalow which is the Mahesh Yogi's (he is rarely in Rishikesh), and the others meditation rooms, offices and a dining room for the disciples. Hidden in the earth is a complex of caves, each a cement chamber lined with stones from the Ganges. The caves are used for meditation. It is stifling hot in the caves—and damp; I remark to the young Australian who is one of the Yogi's assistants that when I stand in the cave I can touch all the walls on all sides. "It's better to meditate in a small space," he says. "The vibrations are better. Instead of shooting off they are turned inward." However, I get a feeling of claustrophobia. I ask the Australian if the Mahesh Yogi is a saint or a god. "You can take him any way you wish. I know that he is a saint, a great one." He adds, rather pedantically, "I've been here one and three-quarter years."

He tells me that the disciple—called a *chela* in India—is given a *mantra*, or sound syllable, to meditate upon. Selection of the proper mantra for the chela is a science, a very difficult one, as there are perhaps millions of possible mantras, and chela and mantra must be properly paired. The Australian says, though, that when the chela receives his mantra, he will know by instinct that it is the correct one. In meditation, the chela concentrates upon the mantra, repeating it to himself over and over; then the mantra leads to deeper concentration, in ever-intensifying circles. He tells me that there are 15,000 teenagers in America practicing the kind of meditation taught by the Maharishi. "We have found that they go off drugs once they begin to meditate. In fact, we will not take anyone who is on drugs." The Maharishi has 500 teachers in the States alone. Where is he now? I ask. "Oh, he is in America. He spends most of his time there. Or else Europe. He is preparing for a big conference in Mallorca. Five thousand teachers will be there."

As we walk down the hill from the meditation caves, five healthy young Westerners appear in the distance, red-faced from carrying their packs in the heat. "Oh, my god," says the Australian. The foreigners drop exhausted into a row of chairs on the roadway and in heavy Swedish accents begin to bombard the Australian with questions. He looks helpless. I slip away and go down the hill through the jungle. I can see the Ganges below me, glistening in the afternoon sun as she flows between the boulders. There are sadhus sitting on various rocks, and in the distance I hear the tinkle of temple bells and the deep boom of gongs, and the air is sweet with the smell of wild flowers, pine, and cow-dung cooking fires.

Hardwar, fifteen miles farther down the Ganges, becomes a virtual city during the pilgrim periods, when tens of thousands of people from all over India come to bathe in the Ganges. The town, which has a normal population of 70,000, was originally known as Kapilastan (the place of Kapila), after the rishi of that name. Kapila spent years in meditation on this part of the Ganges. However, the town was also known, as a tourist pamphlet points out, as Mayawati, Gangadwar and Tapovan. In the central part of Hardwar is a white marble statue of Shiva with a fountain of water splashing playfully on his head.

Hardwar is the site of periodic religious gatherings known as *kumbh* or *kumbha*. They are held all along the Ganges and other rivers. Some are celebrated in twelve-year cycles, as is the greatest of all, at Allahabad, where the Ganges is joined by the Jumna and the Sarasvati, attracting as many as five million people. The gathering at Hardwar, known as Ardh Kumbh, is held every six years.

Everywhere one looks, one sees pilgrims in study or in meditation. This group sits by water's edge in a small temple at Hardwar.

The reason for kumbha, my rather untrustworthy guidebook reports, is this:

It is said that when Surs (gods) and Asurs (Demons) jointly churned the ocean, a pitcher of Nectar came out of it besides 13 other precious items. It was considered that nectar should not be given to Demons otherwise they would become a source of permanent nuisance and trouble to Holi souls. As such, Jayant (son of Indra) took the nectar pitcher and ran away. While running with it nectar drops fell at four places. Hardwar—Prayag—Ujjain and Naisk and a Kumbh fair is held at all these places after 12 years in routine and after 6 years a Ardh Kumbh fair is held at all these places.

There is a yearly kumbh in Delhi on the Jumna in the late fall, and another in January on Sagar Island at the mouth of the Ganges below Calcutta, where the river is known as the Hooghly.

The most sacred site at Hardwar is the Har Ki Pairi, which is one of the spots where the sacred nectar fell. Har Ki Pairi is a bathing site; the water runs into a pool between the shore and a small artificial island which is marked by a huge clock tower, the gift of an Indian industrialist. Because of the confined space, the water speeds by with an uncommon ferocity, and the pilgrims are forced to hang on to chains anchored in the steps when they bathe.

The Ganges canal begins right above the town, so what the pilgrims bathe in is not the true river, which flows a third of a mile away in a feeble stream, but an artificial version of it. There are

A woman who has just bathed in the Ganges at Hardwar dries her hair in the sun.

broad esplanades along both banks of the canal where the pilgrims bathe and pray. The eastern, or left bank as one goes south, is virtually bare of buildings, but the western bank is crammed full of houses and temples, some touching the water. The houses are tightly packed, and the temples seem to be squeezed between them, with their pointed steeples rising as if they had no firm ground for support. The water is still blue here and rushes by swiftly, touching doorsteps and windows. The image I received immediately and retain is that of an Indian Florence, because at this point the Ganges canal bears a strong resemblance to the Arno. Hardwar itself has an Italianate look, at least along the canal. The colors are strong, deep reds, bright greens, accented with peeling whites; trees shoot up from crevices, and the air is crisp and clear, except in the summer when the sky is hot and the heat unbearable. Then the town is overwhelmed with odors. In the late fall and winter the air becomes clear again.

At Hardwar the temperature of the water runs from cool to near freezing. But even in winter the pilgrims immerse themselves in the Ganges as if they were dropping into a tepid bath. I have put my hands and feet in the river at Rishikesh and Hardwar in November and found it impossibly cold, and yet next to me were pilgrims, absorbed in prayer, slowly lowering themselves, some fully clothed, into the eddies along the ghats as if they were in limpid pools instead of a mountain torrent.

As I walk around Hardwar, towering overhead is the crescent of Lord Shiva, balanced on a thin iron rod. Sometimes a red banner flies below the crescent. On buildings is the word OM, sign of the eternal, the primordial sound. In the bazaar are hundreds of tiny stalls, selling red powder for pilgrims to use in their sacrifices, and statues of the gods, conch shells and lingams (the phallic symbol which represents the god Shiva), red and yellow prayer shawls, and beautiful heavy brass pots and bowls. Cows, which are sacred as a symbol of the Eternal Mother, walk about freely through the narrow lanes; and monkeys, which are also sometimes sacred, run along the gutters of the buildings and have terrible squabbles with each other. At the Har Ki Pairi someone has given large flat wheat cakes—called *chapattis*—to the cows, but the monkeys run down and steal them and then leap away chattering angrily.

I walk about the esplanade. The holy men cut great figures: gaunt, sharp-eyed, with long beards, hair knotted on top of their heads; they carry staves with the sharp trident of Shiva. There are beggars all over, cripples and old people and children who drop on the ground and touch one's feet. On the edge of the esplanade, two monks in orange robes are feeding the very poor, who sit in two jagged rows on the ground with metal bowls. As the food is ladled out—it looks like rice and a few vegetables—cows and pariah dogs rush up and fearlessly attack the bowls. There is a lot yelling and shouting, but

Many pilgrims like to practice austerities, such as this man standing for hours on one leg. Others will keep their arms outstretched for days at a time, or sit naked in winter.

one rarely hits a sacred cow. Meanwhile the river flows by in a cleansing rush. I cross the bridge to the other side. Coming directly toward me is a group of men. They look well fed, well clothed, prosperous, fat, except that one of them is stark naked, signifying that he has thrown off *all* earthly attachments.

Across the river is a heavily wooded park, and beyond that, a patch of forest. There are several dozen sadhus camped here, each one alone, huddled over a tiny fire and staying immobile for hours. There is one pair whom I have walked by for several days, and finally I decide to try to talk to them. They are squatting under a huge tree, with their backs against a big log. There is a small fire before them, but they look numb from the cold. They nod to me as I squat down next to them, but I can see that conversation is going to be difficult. They appear to be Sikhs, since they are wearing turbans and iron wrist bangles, the signs of the warrior religious sect that appeared in the Punjab in the sixteenth century when a man named Nanak tried to transcend the religious differences that pitted Hindus and Muslims against each other. I say in my broken Hindi, *"App Punjabi hain?"* They nod slightly and stare at me over the edges of their worn blankets. *"Sikh Saddhu?"* *"Sikh,"* says one of them. Both are heavily bearded; they look ferocious but cold and hungry. I feel

A gathering of holy men meet under a huge shamiana (a type of roofed tent). They wear shawls proclaiming in Sanskrit Shri Ram, or Lord God, in large red letters.

that I should have brought some food. We sit for a long time in silence. I can't tell if they are in meditation or merely cold. Finally I leave.

At one time the mountains around Hardwar were full of wild animals —elephants, tigers, leopards, wolves, the Indian lion, and wild dogs. Today the jungle holds nothing more dangerous than bear and antelope and some American hippies who have found caves alongside the older hermits and rishis. Because the area is empty, the central government considers it a good place for industrialization, and thus hopes to de-emphasize the heavy concentration of factories around the major cities.

Right below Hardwar is a pharmaceutical plant, with its own company town, looking antiseptic, prim and somewhat shoddy. The biggest project, three miles east of Hardwar, is Bharat Heavy Electricals, which manufactures motors, turbines, generators and similar items. The factory, which is slowly being constructed, is sponsored by the government but owned by a single family, who also have four other plants. A young member of the family is staying at the guest house; he appears at meals in his bathrobe, because it is so cold. He tells me that they will eventually have 20,000 workers. He has just married a girl picked out by the family and is anxious to return home. I wonder what will happen to Hardwar when the factory is finished, since each worker will presumably be one of a family of four or five people. There are certain to be major changes in the town when the population is increased by another hundred thousand or so.

I had come to Hardwar by bus, but going back to Delhi I took the auto service, which is quicker—if one has nerves of steel. Our driver ran down a cyclist, an aged man on a battered bike. We dropped the victim off at an army hospital, with no exchange of names or information, and continued our mad dash. There were four other passengers, one of them a fat swami with a shaved head, wearing the orange robes of the holy man. I began to talk to a young man in Western clothes. He had come up to Hardwar to consign the bones of a relative to the Ganges. The family does not do this directly: the bones or ashes are given to a *pandit*, a kind of priest, who says mantras over them before immersing them in the river. "Hardwar is a very sacred place," said the young man. "If you cannot die there you must at least be buried there."

On the way down to New Delhi we passed through dozens of tiny villages. It is an impressive area; the road itself is wide and solidly built (there are no superhighways in India, as the West knows them) and lined with huge shady trees. Most of the houses were built of brick and were large and well tended. There were fat oxen standing in the courtyards munching hay, and fat, bright-eyed, active children, and chickens and goats running about. The women, lean, muscular and graceful from their work in

the fields, were richly dressed in bright saris, and wore thick silver anklets and bracelets, the method by which a peasant not only adorns his wife but keeps his wealth. There were great golden fields of wheat lying on all sides and beyond them huge factories with slender smoke-stacks pouring out black pollutants. ("We need more pollutants, not less," someone said to me.) I have seen a lot of India — much of it is distressingly poor — but in this part of the Ganges plain, I was impressed by the richness of the land and the industry of the people. This is the upper part of the Doab, and has tra-ditionally been known to be wealthy and fertile, and thus the object of invading armies and the prize of the Moghuls, the Turco-Persian rulers of India.

On the open plain the villages have an archeological look, as if they had been built four thousand years ago. Some go back a long time, but the inhabi-tants' memories are vague, and there are few records. Other villages are quite new, but the heat, dust and monsoons give everything a long lived-in look. There are standard methods of building: the richer villages may bring in stone or brick, or these may be the common local materials; other houses are built of mud or bamboo or thatch. Mud is common, often in the form of the kind of brick

Endless work is the lot of the poorer peasant. Here, farm women fill in a road on the plain, carrying the earth in baskets on their head.

known in the American Southwest as adobe, or it is often used as a coating over thatch or woven walls. Exteriors may be covered with more mud, or with cow dung, which loses its odor with the passage of time and becomes antiseptic. The floors of some houses are stone or tile, but the common house has nothing but earth or cow dung. In many villages the rich man's house will be no better than that of the poor, because he fears being singled out by *dacoits*, or robbers. On the other hand, I have visited homes that were the equivalent of mansions or small castles, with huge courtyards, large quarters for various branches of the family, and extensive barns. Most Indians, at least in the countryside, live in what is called the joint or extended family, and some families may have fifty to a hundred members.

In the Doab one is struck by the prosperous appearance of the villages, but as one gets onto the plain many of the villages have a mean, downtrodden look. They are made of mud and thatch, and crumble when the Ganges and her tributaries flood. Only the temples, which are built of stone and whitewashed, remain untouched, but even they tend to become undermined by the swirling waters, and some tilt wildly after years of buffeting.

By the time the Ganges has passed through Uttar Pradesh, the biggest and perhaps the most prosperous state, and has entered Bihar, the landscape has changed to one of poverty and famine, which is relieved only by the brief period of the monsoon rains and the floods, when man and beast try desperately to make up for past, present and future deprivation. In Bengal, where the Ganges breaks up into its Mouths, the land is inundated with water. It burgeons with dense vegetation. The villages are often built of brick, and the roofs may be tiled. Tiny canals run along the roads. Elaborate fish traps of finely woven bamboo, fat water buffalo and lush green rice paddies give the land an air of opulence, but Bengalis claim (as do Biharis) that nevertheless theirs is the poorest part of all India.

The British, when they were firmly committed to harnessing the Ganges, made a number of useful studies of the ecology of the river and the plain. They discovered, for example, that in the middle Ganges alone, at a town called Ghazipur, one third of a billion tons of silt was deposited annually. Yet this gigantic mass of upriver farmland made hardly an impression. A British engineer who made the estimate said in his study that, "It is scarcely possible to present any picture which will convey an adequate conception to the mind of the mighty scale of this operation, so tranquilly and almost insensibly carried out by the Ganges."

At Hardwar, after a drop of 12,800 feet, where the river is diverted into the canal, the Ganges proper flows in a mere trickle through great heaps of boulders and stones. I walked along the empty beds feeling that Mother Ganges had been cheated, as if something of her sanctity

Dawn is a sacred moment along the river. From one end to the other people come down to her banks to watch the sun punch a hole in the dawn-gray sky.

and her power had been stolen by the engineers. Hardwar is twelve hundred miles from the Bay of Bengal as the Ganges flows, but only twelve hundred feet above sea level, so that the rate of descent is a foot a mile. This near-flat descent makes the river exceptionally vulnerable to floods. Once the monsoon rains have struck and the banks are breached the Ganges has virtually no fixed course, and the land for miles is inundated with silt from upriver. This flatness has a devastating effect on the course of the Ganges.

Towns and cities formerly situated on the banks of Mother Ganges may awake after the floods, or even realize in the course of the years, that the river is no longer at their door. The Ganges has an urge to wander. One of the first British trading posts established in 1658 at the town of Kazimbazar retains only a pool of water hyacinth as a memory of the Ganges. Rajmahal, the ancient capital of Bengal, was abandoned by the river in the middle of the last century. The Ganges eventually returned, but meanwhile Rajmahal had died as an important center, and now other towns claim precedence. This errant course of the Ganges is marked throughout her length, even on the upper reaches, where her course is more firmly carved. "The stream has a far from stable course," noted a British report issued in 1909 at Saharanpur in the United Province. "The course of the river Ganges is liable to change owing to the shifting of the riverbed," is a common footnote on maps, if a near-accurate one can be found (India is nerv-

ous about maps, due to her immense conflicts with her neighbors, Pakistan and China).

The Ganges canal is a remarkable feat of engineering. It was conceived by Captain Proby Cautley of the Bengal Engineers, who saw the need to divert some of the Ganges' waters to irrigate the lands of the Doab, which suffered from periodic famines. The Moghul princes Babar and Akbar had built a canal earlier in the Doab. The East Jumna Canal constructed in the eighteenth century had been extremely successful in combating famine conditions, and the Doab had become the granary of the Moghuls. "Under Akbar the area under cultivation," says a later historian, "and the revenue from it were far larger than was assessed for the British in 1900." This suggests that Akbar's tax agents were either more skillful than the British or that the latter were defrauded by their own agents.

Cautley made his first survey in 1836, but as he worked—the land was largely unmapped—he found that the course he was charting led him into high escarpments. A severe famine in 1837 and 1838 convinced the East India Company, which then controlled much of India, that the canal was an urgent necessity;

The Har Ki Pairi is a sacred island formed by the Ganges canal at Hardwar. Here, full-clothed pilgrims immerse themselves in the ice-cold rushing stream.

crops had failed and the dead numbered thousands. Cautley started afresh, and digging eventually began in 1842. Because of the nature of the land there are places where the canal crosses other waterways via aqueducts, like roads passing each other in a maze of superhighways. At one intersection, the canal crosses another river, the Solnai, on an aqueduct two and three-quarter miles wide. The canal was completed against terrible hazards including a shortage of funds; a war against the Sikhs in the adjoining province of the Punjab which drained the East India Company energies; and flash floods from neighboring streams in the rainy seasons which filled the canal bed with silt. There was no railway system from Calcutta (the seat of the Company), and materials were brought to the construction sites with the greatest difficulties. Rains destroyed unbaked bricks and even the kilns in the winter of 1850–51. Equipment sent from England, notably a steam engine, was incorrectly designed, and alterations had to be done on the spot.

The first part of the canal was completed in 1854, and water was let into it at Hardwar in April. Construction continued and sections were opened up piecemeal, until by the 1880's the canal finally culminated at Allahabad, at the intersection of the Ganges herself and the Jumna. With the canal in operation, the Doab never was in need of water again, and the day of great famines in this part of India had ended.

Prehistory
The Aryans

Not long ago it was commonly believed that the Aryan invaders of India came upon nothing but primitive tribes, whom they killed, dispersed or absorbed. The more wily tribal peoples supposedly escaped by going south or fleeing into the jungles. However, the true picture is completely different; the Aryans attacked not savages but a highly civilized people, who were on the level of the civilizations of Babylonia, Assyria, and Bronze-Age Greece. The first fragmentary knowledge of this ancient Indian world came in 1922 when an Indian archeologist, Mr. R. D. Bannerji, who was digging in the ruins of a second-century Buddhist temple in Sind (now split between West Pakistan and India), came across some older ruins.

Excavations were begun under the direction of Sir John Marshall, the Director-General of Archeology for India. As Marshall dug deeper, he uncovered a highly complex city, which was given the name of Mohenjo-daro and is believed to have begun to flourish about 3500 B.C., reaching a peak about a thousand years later and continuing on a high level for another thousand years until it met a sudden end. Mohenjo-daro was laid out on a north-south, east-west axis. The main street is thirty-three feet wide and has so far been traced for half a mile. The side streets are about sixteen feet wide. Building was done with burned brick set in a mortar of sand; no stone was used. Some of the buildings, which invariably open upon the main street, were apparently several storeys high. An unusual feature was the presence of bathrooms and a drainage system of pottery pipes leading into street sewers, a system which was far in advance of anything in later-day India and Pakistan. A huge public bath twenty-three by thirty-nine feet has also been discovered, abutting a large building some 100 by 200 feet, which may have been the royal palace.

The townspeople had reached a high level artistically. Although Sind is now very arid and barren and almost treeless, numerous amulets and other objects of bronze showed the presence of jungle animals like tigers, elephants, antelopes, buffaloes, crocodiles and rhinoceri. Designs of Brahmin bulls have been discovered but not those of ordinary cows, nor of horses, for reasons not yet known. There are also a variety of clay figures, carvings in stone and other materials of people, and toys in burnt clay, among them animals with movable parts. Pottery is fine and varied, and was mass-produced in factories. The people were skilled metalworkers. Gold, silver, bronze and lead were some of the materials used. Saws, chisels, knives, razors and other implements have been uncovered. Marshall found works in imported stone which would be considered highly sophisticated in later ages and drew the conclusion that much of present-day Indian culture stems from the civilization of Mohenjo-daro.

Mohenjo-daro is located in the Indus valley, and smaller sites from the same period have been found throughout the valley. However an equally large twin city, Harappa, has been discovered 400 miles away. Excavations so far indicate that the Mohenjo-daro — Harappa civilization probably covered an area extending from the Sumerian border, roughly today's Iraq, to the edge of the Himalayas, where Tibet begins. This civilization came to an end for a number of reasons, one being that the water level of the Indus valley had begun to rise, thus flooding out some cities and weakening the foundations of walls and houses in others, especially Mohenjo-daro. The people apparently had attained a relatively lasting peace because, despite the high quality of other tools, their weapons were definitely inferior. When the weakened and peace-loving cities fell to the invading Aryans, this great culture continued on a peasant level. Sind, which was once a well-watered, fertile, densely populated land with a pleasant climate, eventually turned into a desert as the result of a series of climatic changes that affected central Asia and northwestern India.

Marshall found a number of elements that survive in contemporary India. Among them are two-wheeled carts, river boats, techniques of pottery making and of casting metal, architecture, the turban, and the use of eye shadow called *kohl.* But even more important was the tracking down of certain religious and mythological elements in the Indus civilization which, Marshall believed, was "so characteristically Indian that it can hardly be distinguished from Hinduism." Along with the cult of the Great Goddess—who emerges later as Mahadevi, or Kali, or Parvati, or Uma—and a god who is to become Lord Shiva, Marshall found animal worship, phallic worship (today a most common rite in India) and the cult of trees, groves and water, which are also popular religious forms in contemporary Hinduism. Such practices were absent in the religious practices of the Aryan invaders. One of the most interesting discoveries is that of figures of yogis seated in meditation in the now-famous lotus position.

But this civilization did not remain static. It eventually spread to the Ganges plain, where it attained an even higher level. When Alexander the Great invaded western India in 326 B.C., he learned of the veneration paid to the Ganges and commented upon it. The Greeks also mentioned the institution of caste, the system which divides mankind into four major groups or ranks and a multitude of minor ones. The core of Indian life and thought, the very essence of being Indian, had already been established. Yet this invasion, which is one of the landmarks of Western history, is no more than a momentary breeze in India. An encounter which echoes throughout our past gained not a single word in Indian records, for—surprising thought for the Westerner—Indians have virtually no interest in detailed written history. What Indians know of the past is the record of the gods and the sacred, of a cosmic world which is reflected in India, which is not only past and present but future as well. For unlike the West, which progresses in a linear route, Indian thought, or Hindu thought, tends to circular and cyclical patterns. What has happened will happen again. Some knowledge of the past shines dimly through ancient religious works, such as the *Vedas*, *Upanishads* and the *Mahabharata*, which are more or less comparable to the Bible.

The *Rig-Veda*, an earlier work, and one of the most graphic and greatest of the Aryan epics, tells about vast battles with people known as the Asyurs, whom scholars took for a long time as mythical creatures, or at best, primitive beings who fell before the superior Aryans. The Aryan scriptures speak of lowly black people who died in bloody battles, whose forts, which Western scholars translated as mere earthworks, were the high ramparts of Mohenjo-daro and Harappa. The *Rig-Veda* is in actuality the battle report and body count of conquerors who despised the conquered. The ancient writings are still so much a part of ordinary human life that their historical authenticity has been questioned only by foreigners and a few Westernized Indians. For the main part these scriptures stem from actual events, which took place either along the Indus or on the Ganges plain.

The first Western research into Indian scriptures was for the purpose of linguistics study, with fierce battles between one Sanskrit scholar and another over minute shades of meaning. It is now apparent, however, that there is substantially more in these works than an early form of the Indian languages disguised as folklore or myth. The scriptures contain the core of Indian thought and religious belief. Studied in the proper perspective they also reveal a certain amount of historical information. However, there is nothing in them of the character of Thucydides' *History of the Peloponnesian War* or the works of other early Greek historians. Nor are there biographies similar to *Plutarch's Lives*.

The Western scholars who opened up the treasures of India for the most part never visited India, preferring to work at home in the comfort of their studies with texts that reached Europe through haphazard circumstances.

Thus Max Müller, a German scholar highly respected in India today as a symbol of the best of Western scholarship, made extensive annotated translations of the *Upanishads*. An American, Irving Babbitt, translated the *Dammapada*, one of the seminal Buddhist works, from the Pali, a language of eastern India in Buddha's time; though like Müller he never visited India. Müller, who was personally ignorant of everyday India and the East, said of Eastern religious works that "They can never be judged from without, they must be judged from within." He added, "We cannot separate ourselves from those who believed in these sacred books." He believed that "We need not become Brahmans or Buddhists or Taosze altogether, but we must for a time, if we wish to understand."

Müller had perhaps an unconscious feeling of European "superiority" over

A Muslim observatory at Benares tracks the course of the stars, the sun and moon, and shows the seasons, all through the means of gigantic stone implements.

the East; he stated that "Our powers of perceiving, of reasoning, and of believing may be more highly developed" than the Indians, a judgment he made without actual experience or knowledge. He had a low opinion of Indian and other non-European works in general, with remarks about disinterring "from a heap of rubbish some solitary fragments of pure gold." He expressed the hope that the readers of his translations will learn "how to discover some such precious grains in the sacred books of other nations, though hidden under heaps of rubbish."

Müller is a rather typical example of Western thinking about India in the nineteenth century. His was an intellectual's view, but on the practical, everyday level, the attitude was the same, and the results, as we will see, were disastrous. Western understanding of the cultural, historical, artistic and philosophical treasures of India has been slow to come. The first translation of the *Upanishads*, one of the most profound of the world's scriptures, into a "Western" language was made in Persian by Dara Shukoh, the son of the man who built the Taj Mahal. Fifty *Upanishads* were translated, with publication in 1657, and were then translated into Latin by a Frenchman and published in Paris

The adoration of the goddess Durga, who is worshipped every fall by means of painted clay statues (which are then dumped into the Ganges), impressed Europeans (unfairly) as another example of superstition.

in 1802. At that time Persian was the most widely read language of the East and was understood by many European scholars, along with Latin, Greek and Hebrew. Müller complains that the Latin translation was written in so unintelligible a style that it required "lynx-like perspicacity of an intrepid philosopher to discover a thread through such a labyrinth." A philosopher did work his way through the maze: the German, Arthur Schopenhauer, who said that their reading "has been the consolation of my life, and will be of my death," and called them the "products of the highest wisdom." Müller noted that Schopenhauer had "the courage to proclaim to an incredulous age the vast treasures which were lying buried beneath that fearful jargon."

The point that I am trying to make is not only that did very few Westerners make an effort to disengage themselves of their natural conceptions and prejudices, but that history as we know it has no relevance for the Hindu. What is known of Indian history comes largely through the work of others, first of all the Greeks, who saw only a small corner of it, and then various travelers, Byzantine, Chinese, Arab and Persian; and then the Turks, Afghans and Moghuls, who were all Muslims and shared the general linear view of life with the West. The Moghuls, who were invaders, were interested in events, in happenings, in people as people, in a reality one could touch instead of imagine as with the Hindu. For them people were alive.

We know virtually nothing of the

Hindu and Buddhist kings, seers and philosophers and the common people, but with Muslim emperors like Akbar, who kept a journal, India suddenly becomes a part of a world of sights, smells, sounds and the vibrating pulse of daily life. The ancient Indian past has been constructed from archeological excavations and from the evidence found in the scriptures and other works, analyzed, sifted and interpreted. Some additional information comes from the lives of the Buddha, who lived in the sixth century before Christ, and in certain manuals, like those written to instruct statesmen in their conduct of office, and in other books written for the pleasure of the married which include descriptions of the life of the well-to-do.

A case can be made for Max Müller's kind of scholarship on the ground that the scholar must be removed and objective. But how much is missed, when one never walks the streets of an Indian city, or smells it, or sees the people in their poverty and their riches, in their hospitality and their despair; when one never has wandered about the flat countryside, or been stranded by a flood, or spent nights in remote villages with people whose way of life is contemporary with the Babylonians and Assyrians. And who, above all, has never seen the great Mother Ganges at sunrise and in the heat of day, and especially at dusk, when

All along the Ganges, season after season, great melas are held in the honor of Hindu saints and gods. This mela is being celebrated on the Yumna, a Ganges tributary.

the cattle walk along the sandy banks prodded by children twisting their tails, while the river herself is full of life, with leaping porpoises and birds swooping low, and clouds of insects swarming about one's head and arms and feet. Then the obscurities of the Scriptures, the personification of Word, Thought, Fire, Water and Ether become alive.

Explorations of the ancient civilizations of the Doab and the Gangetic plain are still in the early stages. Only rudimentary knowledge exists of the beginning stages of civilization in these areas. To date, some three dozen sites have been excavated, mostly in the Doab or in the area west of Calcutta. A distinctive series of hoards of copper objects have been found which extend from the Doab into Bengal. The objects fall into two major categories, either tools—ax heads, chisels, fishhooks and harpoon heads—or weapons—spearheads and swords, and an unidentified long weapon which might be either. A distinct type of statuette, presumably an anthropomorphic figure, sometimes as tall as eighteen inches, has also been found at various sites. However, the purpose of the figurines, which seem to be representations of men with straddled legs and curved arms, is obscure. The probable dates for the copper objects and the figurines found alongside them is about 1700 to 1000 B.C.

The message of the objects to archeologists and anthropologists is that they were created by a semi-nomadic people, who cleared jungle areas for minor agriculture but lived primarily by hunting and fishing and moved along the plain to other sites when necessary. There are still jungle people in India today, commonly called Avidasis, or in the Western term, tribals, who live in the same manner. The tribals come from a number of backgrounds: some are the descendants of the people driven away from the Indus by the Aryans, others are true aboriginals, and still others are various types of Mongoloid people. The Avidasis number some fifty million people, about eight percent of India's population.

The copper culture spanned an area of some 800 miles, indicating that trade and trade routes were established early. One archeologist, not wanting to commit himself to attempting to postulate an elaborate culture, stated that "All that can safely be said is that the copper implements are shown, by their frequency, specialized character and skillful casting and hammering and by their distribution over 800 miles of jungle landscape, to have been the work of substantially whole-time experts who were probably also (as in other parts of the world) itinerant."

Immediately upon the heels of this copper civilization, but at a date still undetermined, there came a highly evolved and widespread urban culture. It seems to have appeared spontaneously, and the historical and archeological origins are unknown. Evidence of this culture has been found in a number of sites along the Ganges plain. One site that has been rather thoroughly exca-

A young Bengali celebrates the feast of Diwali, a festival of lights in which presents are exchanged and people do a lot of party-going. It is one of the most popular of the numerous Indian fêtes.

vated and is typical of others is a city called Hastinapura in the Upper Doab. The occupation layers at Hastinapura are four in number, the earliest being defined by a rough ochre-colored pottery which has been found in other sites.

The second phase has recognizable signs of civic life, because of the remnants of mud-brick walls or unbaked adobe. The pottery, a hard and distinctive gray-painted work with black linear patterns, is known formally as Painted Gray Ware. Copper was still being worked at this time but rarely iron. Animals had been domesticated. Among them the humped bull, buffalo, sheep and pigs. Rice as a cultivated grain had appeared. The date for Period II at Hastinapura is roughly 1000 to 500 B.C. and is the beginning of what may be called the urban period of Indian life, when literature was attaining epic form, theories of government and administration were being developed, and religion, which already had been set into ritualistic, hierarchical moulds was being challenged by two popular folk movements, Jainism and Buddhism, both of which, in different ways, simplified and refined Brahmanic Hinduism, making it easily accessible to the masses.

Period III, from 500 to 150 B.C., is distinguished by the use of iron and the introduction of a system of coinage derived from the Graeco-Persian kingdoms that were established in western India. A new kind of pottery developed, a very distinctive glossy black ware, labeled Northern Black Polished Ware, and appeared throughout the Doab, replacing Painted Gray Ware. The new pottery had the appearance of polished iron. In Period III, bricks were baked and thus achieved a certain permanency and solidity in building. City life became highly sophisticated, and in many respects was quite similar to the life styles of today's Indian towns and villages untouched by Westernizing influences. The land, particularly along the banks of the Ganges and her tributaries, was cleared in large areas. The chiefs and leaders attained the status of kings and emperors. Wars between rival families and states were waged on a grand scale, and contact with other, quite distant lands was established; foreign trade became important and added substantially to the economy. The cities—Pataliputra in particular—grew from villages into great commercial and administrative centers. New cities were founded, some with walls as high as forty feet, with circumferences of three and a half to four miles. The population of India, including the South, at this time was roughly about seventy-five million people. Life was good, exciting, fruitful, challenging, creative. For foreigners, India was the Golden Paradise, and was to remain so for a long time.

The Great Invasions

The mountain barriers to the northwest have rarely protected India from invaders. There are deep-cut passes through which warring armies have come with frightening regularity. The Aryan invasions of thirty-five to forty centuries ago are wrapped in the mists of legend and epic poems, but beginning with the Persians there are a few slim historical records, often in the form of inscriptions on rocks, to connect India with the Middle East. Under Darius the Great, who died in 530 B.C. after a twenty-eight year reign, India was made one of the provinces of the Persian empire, the twentieth and richest, according to the Greek historian Herodotus, who lived later. However, the Persians had conquered only a portion of western India, up to the Indus River. The primitive trade routes followed by merchant caravans were developed into an arterial highway under the protection of the Persian King of Kings. The highway was guarded by fortress cities; some were old towns reconstructed for the protection of the highways, and others were newly built by the Persians.

Early in the fifth century B.C. when Xerxes invaded Greece, some of his troops were Indians on war elephants. In 327 B.C. Alexander the Great, who cut his way through the remnants of the Persian empire, invaded India up to the Indus. India was already known to the Greeks by legend and myth as a land of marvels, among them gold-digging ants, people with no mouths, and others who had ears large enough to serve as umbrellas. After crossing the Indus Alexander was welcomed as an ally by the king of Taxila. Three thousand sheep were slaughtered to feed the Greek army at a great feast, and Alexander and his generals had a number of conversations with Brahmin priests, who were said to be very adamant about maintaining their philosophical positions. The Greeks advanced a few miles further, but then the troops, nervous about being in unknown, limitless lands with a seemingly endless number of enemies, refused to continue and Alexander turned back. The time was late in 325 B.C., but Greek contact with India did not stop at that point. A number of small Greek kingdoms survived in western India, and some of their forces not only penetrated the Doab, but moved across the Gangetic plain as far as the modern city of Patna.

From the Western point of view, Greek influence on India is slight, but interesting. The Greeks, through their Persian subjects, introduced the concept of a monetary system employing coins. Greek religious art, in the form known as Gandharan, after the area in Afghanistan where it developed, initiated the style in which Buddha and the Bodhisattvas are seen: many early Buddhas are hardly more than the Greek god Apollo, even to the shape of the head, face, nose, eyes and the drapery. A Buddhist text known as the *Question of Milander* (or *Menander*) records series of conversations between a Greek general, Menander, visiting the court at Pataliputra and a Buddhist sage. The Sanskrit terms for such words as horse-bit, pen, book and mine are Greek, and Indian astrology and medicine contain Greek terms.

After Alexander, the Greeks continued to make forays into India. The evidence is scanty—some coins and a few slight references in Greek and Indian literature. There is a temptation on the part of the West to romanticize the importance of Greek influence in India, but it is actually minor. Certain cities were laid out on Greek forms, but in general India had little interest in the Greeks, seeing them merely as still another kind of barbarian. Persia, which was a Greek province, carried on a running battle with the great Gangetic state of Maurya for the control of Afghanistan and the Punjab. About 250 B.C. this Greek empire began to fall apart. One group of Greeks remained in the Afghani mountains known as the Hindu Kush; these Greeks, men of unsurpassed courage, now began a new foray into India, pushing steadily south and east, founding small military posts which became kingdoms, only to be swallowed up by the surrounding Indians, as the core band of Greeks moved eastward. The height of the Indo-Greek expansion came in 150 B.C. when the legendary Menander led his men against the great Gangetic city of Pataliputra (now Patna). The city was the capital of Magadha, the largest state of India. Menander's purpose in this expedition is unknown: he may have seen the city as the key to a new Greek empire. At any rate, after a few months, Menander was driven off and he returned to the Punjab. After his death, the power of the Greeks faded, and the survivors retreated to the hills.

Mysterious, brooding, enigmatic: a door to a temple-home overlooking the sacred river.

One of the phenomena of the early invasions of India is that the invaders were often people displaced from their own lands by other invaders, in a kind of bumping process that continued over several centuries. About the middle of the second century B.C., groups of Parthians on the Caspian Sea in the Greek empire began to revolt. They were forced to leave their homes and move southward; in India they pushed out the remnants of the Greek kingdoms. Behind the Parthians (known as Pahlavas in India) came the Sakas, who had been driven out of central Asia by Mongol hordes, the Yueh-chi. In India the Sakas overwhelmed what Greeks remained and either absorbed the Pahlavas or forced them to move again. The Yueh-

chi successes were only temporary, for they were pressed by the Wu-san, and they in turn migrated into India. The Indians called them Kushans. Physically larger and more aggressive than previous nomadic tribes, the Kushans gained control of the region that ran from western Afghanistan to the Gangetic plain, up to Benares; the northern border touched Chinese Turkestan. The Kushans have been described as "big pink-faced men, built on a large scale." They wore long-skirted coats, soft leather boots and had the custom, odd to the Indians, of sitting on chairs rather than the ground. A long period of peace began with the Kushans; they gave great freedom to Buddhism; one of their kings called a general council to establish the canon of holy books for

Buddhism. Today northwest India is still dotted with Buddhist temples and shrines from the Kushan era.

On the eve of the eleventh century, when the Arabs first invaded India, Indian civilization covered an immense arc, from Afghanistan to the South Pacific. A long chain of islands, Ceylon, Indonesia, the Philippines, and New Guinea, as well as Southeast Asia (that is, Indochina—now Burma, Thailand, Laos, Cambodia, Vietnam and Malaya) fell under Indian religious, cultural and economic hegemony. The Indian in-fluence was direct. The great complex of temples at Angkor Wat in Cambodia, in a city that once served a million people (it was empty and covered with jungle when it was rediscovered in the nine-teenth century) was filled with temples dedicated to Shiva. The ruling families bore Indian names, and the social struc-tures of these islands were based on Indian patterns, though the caste system eroded and dissolved when Indians migrated.

In the West, Indian philosophical con-cepts, transmitted through contacts with the Arabs in the Caliphate in Damascus, transformed European thinking in the most subtle of means. Buddhist themes of peace and brotherhood influenced the Middle East as early as the third century before Christ. In fact, one of the early Christian saints, St. Jehoshaphat is none other than the Bodhisattva, Buddha, baptised and Westernized; some of the legends of the saint are exactly the same as those attributed to Buddha 900 years earlier.

Perhaps the most subtly significant gift from India was its system of mathe-matics. The ordinal numbers we com-monly call "Arabic," as opposed to Roman numerals, are actually Indian, and their expression in the ancient Devanagari script, still the common alphabet of northern India, is close to their form as the West still uses them. Indian mathematics have given the world the tools of all scientific calcu-lations. Mathematics developed from the ancient Hindu cosmology as a philo-sophical means of explaining the symbol of Brahman, the Universal Being who is the Center and of Nirvana, the final goal in which man is absorbed in the Center. The primary or final reservoir of all single shapes and numbers is zero, 0, from which come all figures but which is without the limitations of value itself. And zero gives us the decimal point (.), from which all numbers ascend and descend without limit.

Of all the numbers, zero is the most important because it fulfills certain dynamic properties: all positive and all negative numbers are inherent in it. Zero is the transition point between opposites, symbolizing the balance be-tween divergent tendencies. Zero is the All and the None, the matrix of positive and negative, of addition and subtrac-tion, of creation and destruction—con-cepts which run throughout Indian cosmology. Zero is the void, but all the distinct numbers, from one to nine, gain an infinite power of expansion by the addition of this apparent void. Thus without the concept of Indian mathematics, the West would still be counting in terms of I, II, III and so on, to the detriment, we might guess, of our infinitely complex world. But much as the Middle East and the West gained by contact with India, India had no use for the foreigner.

One of the invading Turkish tribesmen of the eleventh century, a man named Alberuni, a great intellectual, wrote in a work (called in English *An Enquiry into India*) that the Hindus had an obsessive hatred for all "barbarians," whom they called *mlechchas*, a term which is still used. Alberuni mentions the Hindus' special pride in their civilization and their contempt for whatever is alien to Hinduism; he lists their reluctance to communicate their culture and knowledge to *mlechchas*. But he also mentions their religious tolerance, and he has contempt for their reluctance to risk their lives for any ideal.

This Hindu isolation and passivity left India open to a great new invasion, unlike anything since the days of the Aryans. The Muslim attack on India that began in the eleventh century was an explosion that echoes even today. The attack began with a central Asian Turkish chief named Mahmud of Ghazni, who had received the sanction of the Caliph of Baghdad for a holy war against the land of India, which, by Muslim standards, was pagan. Alberuni was among his court, and some of what we know about the attacks comes from his writings. Mahmud and his warriors raided India over a twenty-five year period, sweeping down in the cool months, destroying Hindu temples and idols (and Hindus, whom they considered idolators), and returning home with their loot as the oppressive summer heat began to close in upon them. What Mahmud brought back to Ghazni, his home in Afghanistan, was, as one chronicle says, "jewels and unbored pearls and rubies shining like sparks of iced wine, emeralds like sprigs of young myrtle, and diamonds big as pomegranates." In incredible raids with his horses and pack camels, Mahmud ranged wherever he wanted, into the south and across the Doab, beyond Delhi, even attacking Mathura, the city on the Ganges tributary, the Jumna, sacred to the Lord Krishna. Mahmud's followers retained the Punjab, which was to remain heavily Muslim. And they impressed upon Hindus a deep-rooted fear that has survived to the present, a sense of brutal intolerance. The Muslims found the Hindus pagan, but the Hindus saw the new invaders as destroyers of the sacred, of their temples and shrines, and as murderers of their holy people.

Near the end of the twelfth century another Turkish dynasty replaced the

A Hindu saint, Manam Sanpradaya, died after making a prediction of one thousand years of chaos, followed by eternal peace. The rose appeared by his head miraculously after the photograph was taken.

Gaznivids, attacking Hindu India at will. The Turks suffered a major defeat in 1191, but then they destroyed a Hindu army and marched into Delhi, once the sacred city of Indraprastha, and made it their capital. The Gangetic plain offered no great resistance as the enemy marched along the river banks. Benares was sacked in a wild battle that reduced this most sacred city to rubble, and the Turkish advance continued. The Indians were brave warriors—the fighting was done generally by the members of one caste, who were soldiers by tradition—but they were no match for the Turks, who were vigorous, aggressive and fearless. Indian methods of war had hardly changed since Alexander the Great had been confronted fourteen hundred years earlier, but the Turks employed the most modern techniques—archers of marvelous accuracy in massed firepower, and swift, mobile, well-disciplined horsemen—against Indian footsoldiers armed with maces and spears. In a sense, it was modern man against the pre-industrial.

In 1206 the Muslim general Qutb-ud-din Aibak detached India from the rule

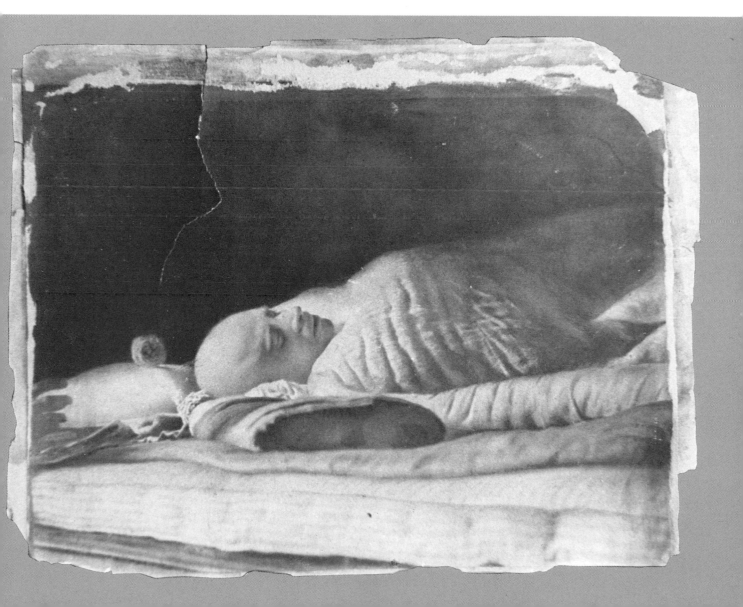

A Sikh seer tells the fortune of an upper-class Bengali woman. She doesn't like what she hears and turns away in anger.

of the parent kingdom in Afghanistan and established himself in Delhi as sultan. He was the first of a series of thirty-four sultans of different dynasties who ruled, more or less successfully, until 1526, when the Moghuls took over. For this period India was ruled by foreigners, by Turks, Afghans, Persians and other Muslims, whose ranks were being continually refreshed by immigrants from the northwest. The Islamic rulers were devout Muslims to the point of fanaticism, intolerant of Hindus and Hindu culture; they were brutal, rapacious, bloody and treacherous. Fellow Muslims were executed as quickly as Hindus. They did encourage the arts to a degree unknown before in India. Music, painting, literature and the minor arts, along with a new type of architecture combining Islamic and Indian styles and magnificent in its imagination and scope developed.

These were exceptional men who attacked and ruled India. An Arab traveler from Morocco, Ibn Batuta, who visited Delhi in 1333, wrote of one sultan: "Mohammed is a man who, above all others, is fond of making presents and shedding blood. His generous and brave actions, and his cruel and violent deeds, have obtained notoriety among the people. The ceremonies of religion are dear to his heart and he is very severe in respect of prayer and the punishment which follows its neglect." This sultan, Mohammed Shah, conspired with an Islamic prophet named Shaik Nizam-ud-din Aulia against his father Tughlaq.

When Tughlaq returned from an excursion against an enemy, he was to pass through a wooden archway, which Mohammed had built in such a way that it collapsed from the heavy tread of his father's elephant. But Mohammed Shah's successor, his cousin, was a more humane man. Like many of the Muslim nobility, he was literate and kept a journal. He was an extensive and creative builder, and of his work he wrote: "Among the many gifts which God has bestowed upon me, His humble servant, was the desire to erect public buildings. So I built many mosques and colleges and monasteries, that the learned and the elders, the devout and the holy, might worship God in these edifices, and aid the kind builder with their prayers." Under the Muslim sultans, Delhi became a magnificent city. An Arab from Damascus gives us a description of it:

Delhi consists of several cities which have become united, and each of which has given his name to all the rest. It is both long and broad, and covers a space of about forty miles in circumference. The houses are built of stone and brick, and the roofs of wood. The floors are paved with a white stone, like marble. None of the houses is more than two storeys high, and some only one. It is only in the Sultan's palace that marble is used for pavement. . . . Delhi comprises an aggregate of twenty-one cities. Gardens extend on three sides of it, in a straight line of twelve thousand paces. The western side is not so furnished, because it borders on a mountain. Delhi contains a thousand colleges [for the religious orders]. There are about seventy hospitals. In the city and its environs, the chapels and hermitages number two thousand. There are great monasteries, large open spaces, and numerous baths.

But this great city was soon to be sacked by another nomad. Shortly before the end of the fourteenth century the notorious Timur, conqueror of Persia, Afghanistan and Mesopotamia, raided India. Most of the country accepted him passively though sullenly, but when he entered Delhi, the large Hindu minority who formed the lower classes and the bulk of the tradesmen, began to defend themselves. In his autobiography the great warrior tells what happened:

The savage Turks fell to killing and plundering. The Hindus set fire to their houses with their own hands, burned their wives and children with them, and rushed into the fight and were killed. The Hindus showed much courage in fighting. The [Muslim] officers in charge of the gates prevented any more troops from entering the city, but the flames of war had risen too high. On that day, Thursday, and all of that night, nearly fifteen thousand Turks were engaged in slaying, plundering and destroying. When dawn broke on Friday, my entire army, no longer under control, went into the city and thought of nothing but murdering, plundering and taking prisoners. The following day, Saturday, was spent the same way and the booty was so great that each man took from fifty to a hundred prisoners, men, women and children. The other spoil was immense: rubies, diamonds, garnets, pearls and other gems; gold and silver ornaments, and brocades and silks of great value.

Timur ordered the craftsmen and artisans to be picked out of the mass of prisoners, and these men he distributed to his nobles and administrators for their courts. When he was finished with Delhi, Timur continued his advance, and the sultan, who had fled, returned to his throne.

Turkish Muslim rule was not terribly stable, or widely accepted. There were numerous offshoots, rebel kings and generals, revolts by the Hindus, palace upheavals, and a general waning in the aggressive energies of the Muslims. The widespread debility of the Muslim states presented a wonderful opportunity for still another Turk from Central Asia. He was Babur, and he was the descendent of the great scourges of Asia, Genghis Khan and Timur. From his youth, when he conquered Afghanistan, Babur wrote in his autobiography, "I had always been bent on subduing Hindustan." He adds: "In the space of seven or eight years I entered it five times at the head of an army. The fifth time the most High God, of His grace and mercy, cast down and defeated an enemy so mighty as Sultan Ibrahim, and made me the master and conqueror of the powerful empire of Hindustan." Unlike other Turks, Babur did not like India. He left no monuments in this country he had fought so hard to

A Sufi—a Muslim mystic—squats on his knees in prayer at the Jama Masjid, the great mosque of old Delhi. The Sufis are a mystical, anti-establishment movement with a great popular appeal among the poor in the East.

A celebration in honor of Muhammad's son-in-law, Ali, brings out great emotion among India's Muslims. Ali was not accepted by more orthodox leaders in the Middle East, and his followers are considered by them as heretics.

win. "Hindustan is a country of few charms," he wrote from his palace in Agra, on the Jumna near its confluence with the Ganges. "Its people have no good looks." Babur was the first of the Moghuls, a dynasty that brought a new vitality to Hindustan. His death is touching. His son, Humayun, was ill, and Babur so feared for the boy's life that he offered God his own in exchange. It is said that God heard his prayer, and the emperor died in 1530, at the age of forty-eight.

Mastery of the Gangetic plain gave the Moghuls control of much of India. At Delhi, at the spot once called Indraprastha—one of India's most sacred

cities because it was here that the five Pandu brothers of sacred legend fought their enemies—the invaders built the biggest of their capitals. It became not just another city, but the center of an empire reaching into Afghanistan on the west and across the plain to Bengal and far into the south. The central part of this area was where Hinduism developed and was the site of the Mahabharata, one of the greatest of the Indian epics. Located here also were tens of thousands of Hindu temples and shrines, including sacred locales such as the birthplace of Lord Krishna and several spots touched by pieces of the goddess Durga falling from heaven. Over the centuries the area was devastated by the Muslims. The holy buildings were largely destroyed, and the stones used as parts of Muslim buildings. Mosques replaced temples. What had been sacred Hindu India became Islamic. All along the Jumna and the Ganges, to Allahabad where the two rivers meet and beyond, through Bihar and deep into East Bengal are great Muslim monuments. A hundred miles east of Delhi is Agra with the Taj Mahal, the one building that for many foreigners symbolizes all of India, which ironically it is not Hindu at all, but Muslim. What seems "Indian," is actually Turkish, Afghan, Persian, even Arab—all, however, Indianized to some extent with great subtlety and sophistication.

But the great Muslim dynasties could not retain their creativity and vitality with the same fervor that brought them to India. Inevitably heat, dust, frustration and the boredom that eventually sears every man who thinks he has conquered India enervated the Moghuls as well. By the eighteenth century the Turks no longer had the capacity to keep their rule alive, and a new enemy was already solidly entrenched in India, an enemy more subtly cruel and destructive, and less sensitive than the Turks. Where the Muslims became Indian, the new arrivals, the English never did. The Turks could enliven and create, absorb and be absorbed, but the English, to the end of their rule were hardly more than parasites on India. It is still too soon to put them into perspective, as we can with the Muslims. The Muslims, sweeping across the vast plain into Bengal, became more Indian from day to day; the British, starting at the far end of the Ganges, became less Indian the longer they stayed.

The Muslims, unlike other invaders who found themselves overwhelmed in India's living mass, came as equals, as a people as advanced as the Hindus culturally, intellectually, religiously. They brought with them fine artistic sensibilities which served as a counterpoint to their high skills as warriors and administrators. Their theology, which formed the inner core of their lives, was as intricate, creative and as sophisticated as Hinduism. The Muslims were literate, intelligent, aggressive, energetic; they sprang from a mature, civilized world which was known from Spain to the South Seas. Islam could not be absorbed or synthesized; it was not a barbaric superstition. Islamic culture soon became dominant on the Indian continent, without, however subduing Hinduism, particularly among the higher castes. Islam had a great attraction for the poor and oppressed, and made a great number of converts. The theme of brotherhood of all men in Islam attracted so many Hindus that soon a quarter of India had become Muslim.

The dichotomy that developed finally split India into two warring factions. This antagonism was used by the British to great advantage when they began to absorb the Indian states. The men in India whom the British found best to work with, on a man-to-man basis, were the Muslims; British India is largely Muslim India. Rudyard Kipling, for example, found that Muslim India was more congenial, and his writings sound as if Muslim India were the true India. This bias also comes out in such works as E. M. Forster's famous novel, *A Passage to India.* The two warring, antagonistic factions of India, have, under the pressure of modern politics, split the country into two sections: India herself, a secular state which is predominately Hindu, and Pakistan, a theocratic Muslim state with a very small Hindu minority. The Partition of 1947, when the two states were formally separated, brought the deaths of millions of people, equal perhaps to all the deaths of World War II, and the exchange of millions of people who preferred either India or Pakistan as a homeland. But the situation has never been resolved: border clashes continued, with several small undeclared wars, the greatest being the tragic conflict of 1971, when the separatist movement in East Pakistan was given military support by India, and the situation threatened to entangle the great nations of the world.

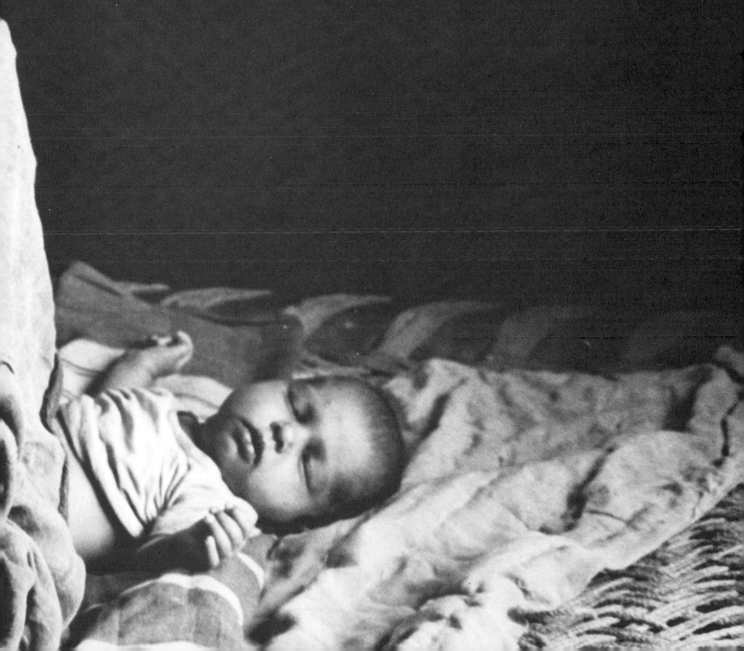

Portraits of India

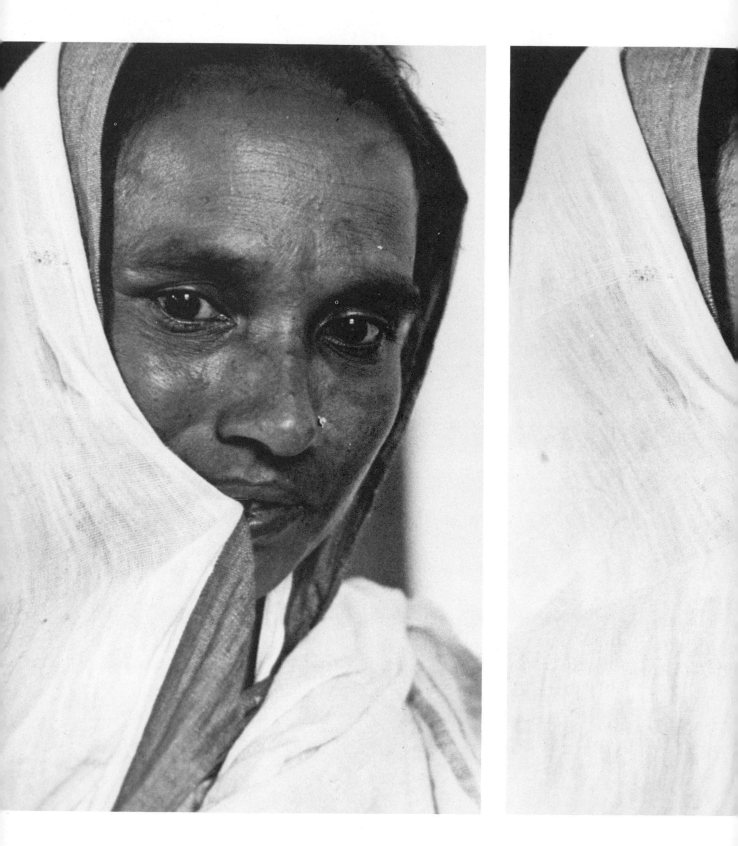

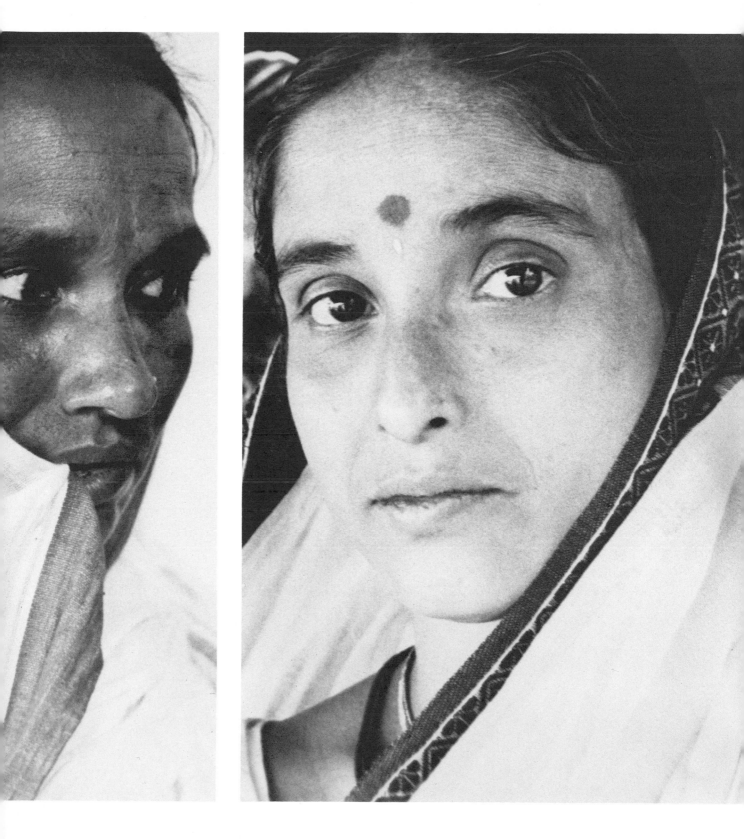

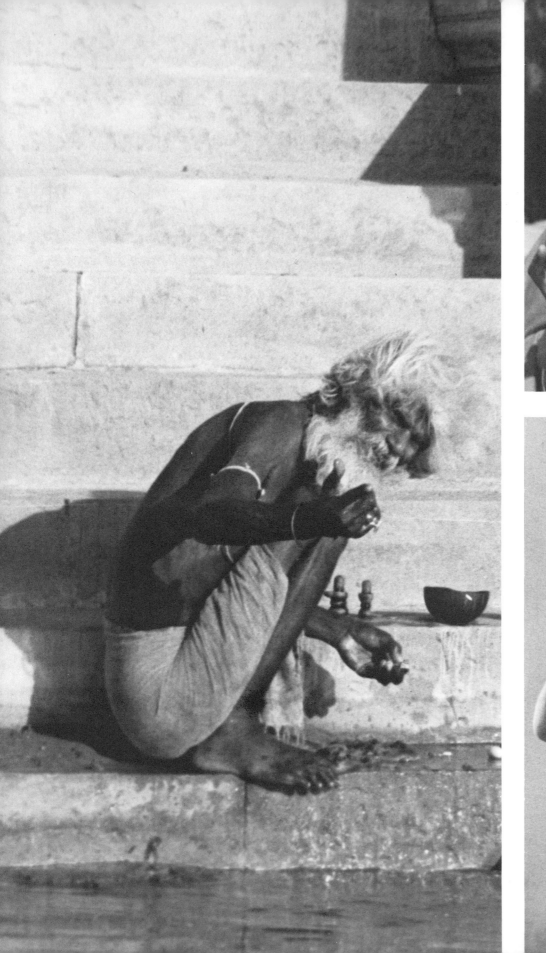

The British Take Over the Ganges Plain

3ritish conquest came in a piecemeal fashion, and was unplanned. It was not considered an easy conquest, most British historians have written about the British invasion of India. Indians, of course, never enjoyed being occupied by foreigners, but their vast land was as easy to cross as the ocean once the mountain barriers had been breached. When the English began to take India, even the already established "foreigners" like the Moghuls were no more enthusiastic about sharing their country than were the Hindus.

The first Europeans to land in India with a view to a long-range stay were the Portuguese who founded trading posts in South India before the Moghul empire was established. Vasco da Gama put a colony ashore in 1498. Twelve years later, Alfonso de Albuquerque, another Portuguese admiral, founded a colony at Goa, which was to remain Portuguese until 1961. The Portuguese, who had highly adventurous and brave admirals, founded small colonies as far away as Indonesia, but lacked the naval strength to maintain them; the Dutch seized many of these outposts. The English, too, were aware of the riches of the East, and in 1600 a group of businessmen, later to be known as the East India Company, received a charter from Queen Elizabeth I which granted them a monopoly of English trade with the "Indies," which included India, China and Indonesia. The Dutch, however, ejected the Company from Indonesia in 1623, and thereafter it concentrated its efforts on India and China. Meanwhile the Danes and the French were busy opening up trading posts in India along the coasts. Late in the seventeenth century, Charles II of England married a Portuguese princess and received the port of Bombay, a great natural harbor on India's west coast, as part of the dowry. Bombay was rented to the Company for a token ten pounds per year. But the Company's most productive property was the port which was to be called Calcutta.

In 1690 the East India Company obtained from the Moghul Emperor Aurangzeb the right to settle on the banks of the Ganges, on a stretch of the river known locally as the Hooghly. Here a fort was built, and a few years later the English rented three small villages from the Nawab of Bengal. Thus, with forts at Bombay, Madras, Cuddalore (a southern town) and Calcutta, the English had taken the step that brought them beyond mere commercial enterprises. They were now unwittingly committed to a policy that demanded more and more intervention into India if they were to maintain their original investments. Soon they had direct control over three-fifths of India, and indirect control over the Indian princes who ruled the remainder of the country. In 1707 Emperor Aurangzeb died, leaving Moghul India in a state of chaos. England and France were at war in Europe and North America, and extended the conflict to India, plotting with and employing Indian princes against each other. The battles dragged on throughout the decades. At first the English suffered reverses, but by the middle of the century a young clerk in the Company named Robert Clive, with a mere 200 English and 300 Indian soldiers, withstood a siege of 10,000 Indian troops under French control. In 1756 Clive suborned a general in an Indian army allied with the French, and with some 3,000 men, less than a third of them English, "defeated" an Indian army of 68,000 troops at the "battle" of Plassey. This victory gave the Company virtually unlimited control of the Ganges plain, with its untapped wealth, natural resources, rice paddies, fields and factories. The British saw before them wealth a man could barely dream of, and they were quick to make the most of their opportunities. The looting of India had begun.

Ironically the East India Company itself hardly profited by the riches that lay open for the taking. The Company's own employees were the gainers. Clive, who was one of the greediest to loot India, was impeached by the English Parliament. In his defense he claimed that in view of the wealth that lay before him, "I was astonished at my own moderation." An ambitious, lonely man, he later committed suicide. Warren Hastings was sent out as the Crown's governor-general to establish some kind of control over the Company, but found himself in a constant and frustrating battle with its members when he tried to affirm that the English privilege in India was not to merely provide a source of income, but also included a responsibility and an obligation requiring understanding, sympathy and good government. Hastings resigned after a few years and was unexpectedly impeached by Parliament for his high-handed treatment of the Indian princes, but he was acquitted. His temporary successor, Sir John Macpherson, did his best to maintain the earlier exploitative traditions, and Lord Cornwallis, his successor, remembered best by Americans as the English general beaten by George Washington at the battle of Yorktown, described Sir John's rule as a "system of the dirtiest jobbery." Cornwallis found that the situation with the Company was completely out of hand. After defeating its own puppet state, Nawab, which had rebelled in a battle in 1764, the Company gained control of Bengal, Bihar and Orissa and was given the right to collect revenues in these states by the Moghul· emperor, who had no actual power over them. Cornwallis made some temporary reforms, but after his retirement conditions reverted to normal.

In 1798 Richard Wellesley was sent out with his brother Arthur, later to become the Duke of Wellington, and the Company's empire building continued. Richard Wellesley thought Indians "vulgar, ignorant, rude, familiar, and stupid," and thus possessing no rights to their own country. He was very open about annexing more and more sections of India, although the English Parliament in its Regulating Act of 1784 had stated, "To pursue schemes of conquest and extension of dominion in India are measures repugnant to the wish, honour, and policy of this nation."

But English policies were inconsistent. At times they favored operating without any changes in Indian customs or institutions, on the theory that the Company could better profit this way. Thus missionaries were forbidden to proselytize because the Company thought they might antagonize the people. Then the Crown ran to the other extreme and tried to go about tidying up India with great and radical innovations. The English were divided among themselves: the Company was in India, firstly and lastly, to make money, to produce dividends for the shareholders. The Crown alternately submitted to this view, and then in contradiction decided exploitation had to stop, seeing England as the civilizing savior of the Indians, eradicating barbarous practices and introducing education and Christianity. The Company cynically thought that reforming India could come to no good and in the end would hurt the Company's interests, but the large numbers of English arriving in India who had no connection with the Company had other views in mind. Wherever the English went they saw practices that offended their English Christian sensibilities: slavery, child sacrifices and child marriages, the burning of widows, the worship of idols. They believed that gross immorality and superstition filled the land.

A critic of both the Company and India, Charles Grant, wrote: "We cannot avoid recognizing the people of Hindoostan a race of men lamentably degenerate and base . . . obstinate in their disregard of what they know to be right, governed by malevolent and licentious passions." And he also complained of the Indians' "great and general corruption of man-

The British came to India and died like flies from heat, disease, the wrong food, war. The old cemetery on Calcutta's Park Street is a tragic memorial to hundreds of English who gave their lives in India in their effort to uphold the Company and the Crown. Many of the young men and women were only in their twenties when they died.

ners." Newly arrived Englishmen and their wives brought with them a reforming zeal to do their "Christian duty" to their little brown brothers. But one of the leading proponents of the status quo, Sir Thomas Munro, commented that he could not share the general faith "in the modern doctrine of the rapid improvement of the Hindoos, or any other people." Munro added that the character of the Hindus was probably much the same when the Portuguese first visited India and was not likely to be any different a century hence. "When I read, as I sometimes do, of a measure by which a large province has been suddenly improved, or a race of semi-barbarians civilized almost to Quakerism, I throw away the book."

But there were destructive practices that had to be abolished, one of them being slavery. In 1772 the English allowed a law to be passed ordering that the families of convicted *dacoits* (or robbers) be sold into slavery, defending it on the grounds that slaves were well treated in India. Two years later Hastings said the law had to be abolished, but it wasn't. In 1785 Sir William Jones, the founder of the Asiatic Society of Bengal, pointed out that almost every man or woman in Calcutta had at least one slave child. Slave boats came down the Ganges to Calcutta filled with children bought from parents during a famine or even stolen. The more humane among the English continued the battle—though the Crown itself, unwilling to alienate the powerful business interests involved in the trade, moved slowly. By the middle

The great Hindu epic, the Ramayana, *performed not in India but in Bangkok. Indian influence penetrated Southeast*

Asia and Indonesia, and the peoples of these areas still retain much of Indian customs, religions and culture.

of the nineteenth century there were sufficiently restrictive laws to cause slavery to gradually wither away.

In 1802 a Baptist missionary learned that Hindu parents were sacrificing their children off the ocean side of Sagar Island in the Ganges delta by throwing them to sharks and man-eating crocodiles in honor of Ma Ganga and the raja's 60,000 sons she had saved from hell. The previous year, twenty-three victims had been offered up. The practice was ordered stopped, but infanticide of baby girls was common practice in many sections of India. The child was usually killed in the room in which it was born by being given a poison from a plant and then being buried in the earthen floor. Sir William Sleeman, the official in charge of eradicating practices the English objected to, wrote that mothers "wept and screamed a good deal when their first female infants were torn from them, but after two or three times giving birth to female infants, they become quiet and reconciled to the usage and say, 'do as you like.'" It was difficult to invade people's homes, particularly at the moment of birth, and the practice continued until close to the twentieth century.

The rite of *sati* (or *suttee*), in which a widow immolates herself upon her husband's funeral pyre, caused the Muslims to pass laws aimed at stopping the practice, but it still continued, and may occasionally take place even today in very remote villages. Sati was practiced primarily among high-caste Hindus. In 1780 the sixty-four wives of the Raja of

Narwar joined him on his pyre, and about the same time a Sikh prince in the Punjab was followed by ten wives and over 300 concubines. The rite was practiced in honor of the goddess Sati, who immolated herself on the pyre of her husband Shiva. Sati, of course, came to life again after this sacrifice, and the very devout Hindu believes the woman who dies in honor of her husband will return to earth in a better, higher form.

Early British attempts to stop sati were ineffectual. In 1803 the Supreme Court in Calcutta, in an evasive ruling, said the government would be well advised to be guided by the religious opinions and prejudices of the natives. In a thirty-year period ending in 1818 the known cases in Bengal more than doubled, perhaps due to better reporting, when 839 instances of sati were listed. It was obvious to the British that, despite their respect for their husbands, a number of Indian women fell on the funeral pyre reluctantly. Some were drugged, others were forcibly tied down by relatives or by the priests. Sati had become a kind of holiday for the villagers, and while it had an ancient religious sanction, it was clear to the authorities that a number of widows were burned by others either in the sheer joy of the festival, or, more practically, to reduce the number of people to share in the dead man's estate.

Completely absorbed in contemplation of the infinite, a Hindu businessman sits in silence at a ghat in Benares. In later years many people enter a life centered around prayer.

Officially sati is long since gone, but in some very obscure, very traditional parts of the country, where there is no contact with the government and the people are very conservative, sati and child sacrifice are probably practiced from time to time. I have seen reports in English-language newspapers in Calcutta and Delhi about child sacrifice, though I suspect that few cases are reported, and if they are, the facts are not made known to the public for fear of offending people.

At the same time they were hoping to stamp out the Indian customs that were abhorrent to them, the English were embarked on a series of drastic Westernizing reforms, among them making English rather than any of the many Indian tongues the official language, and educating likely young Indians for their future role as servants, but not leaders, of the Crown. In 1841 the British had decided not to overlook any "just and honorable accession of territory," a policy which naturally involved them in a wild grab for Indian lands, in which they used every "legal" means (they made the laws, of course) and every illegal means, from bribery, the ousting of legitimate princes and the outright condemnation of Indian titles and rights, to full-scale war. By 1857 they were in complete control of India, either by direct rule or through their puppet princes. India was one great treasure house, and the English drew from her as they wished. But a sudden eruption shook English rule. This was the Sepoy Mutiny, which spread across Hindustan and into the south, effectively welding disparate elements among the

Indians for a short time. It was the beginning of the end, but before I describe the events of the Mutiny, I want to turn to English life in India for a few pages.

From the remote viewpoint of our age, the British in India have a certain charm, if one can forget that they were eagerly, wholeheartedly despoiling an ancient land. Clive told a committee of the British Parliament: "A great prince was dependent on my pleasure; an opulent city lay at my mercy; its richest bankers bid against each other for my smiles. I walked through vaults which were thrown open to me alone, piled on either hand with gold and jewels."

The English attempted to transplant England to India, bringing not only household goods, clothing, their own types of architecture, wines, cuisine, but even vegetables and plants. At the beginning when the Company was being established and there were no English women present, the English were inclined to accept India on Indian terms, wearing Indian clothing, taking Indian women as companions, and living in Indian houses. But as they established their hold, and more and more ordinary civilians came out from England, many accompanied by wives and daughters, Indian customs were abandoned and India became an outpost of England. There is an engraving in a museum in Madras showing new arrivals as they land. They have come by square-riggers, which lie offshore, and are being brought in to the beach by rowboat. They wear waistcoats and cutaways and high black silk hats and must wade the last few steps and get their trousers wet. A lady in a long skirt and a feathered hat, carrying a parasol, is being carried through the surf by two coolies naked except for loincloths.

The English never quite knew how to dress; English women never, for example, adapted the sari, which is lighter and cooler than the heavy clothes foreign women wore in the tropics until after World War I; and most of the English insisted on wearing *topis*, or sun hats, which are made of cork and are extremely heavy, hot and uncomfortable. It took the English a century or more before they learned that heavy meals of meats and puddings with wine were as dangerous as the sun and cholera. Even today, the English who have remained in India, and the Indians who want to be Westernized, eat the most appalling and indigestible foods—heavy roasts, soggy dumplings, overcooked vegetables, sodden puddings and sweets—as if they were still in a land blasted by chilling winds from the Atlantic.

Every major city and town in India, Pakistan and Bangladesh still retains its Civil Lines, which is the former British area. Here are country churches in Gothic styles, parks (called *maidans* in India), English mansions and government buildings in classical styles developed by Christopher Wren and his successors. European influence permeates contemporary India. The Portuguese introduced tobacco, maize, and the potato, which are now staples. They also brought the art of the miniature painting, thus intro-

ducing a form of art into the Indian courts which developed along Persian-Indian lines with great sophistication and charm. The British left better roads, railways, Anglo-Saxon jurisprudence, English as still another language among the seventeen major tongues and 2,000 dialects, and a derogatory feeling among upper-class Indians toward their own people, culture and land. On the other hand, aside from the vast wealth that England took without permission, the British learned the delightful custom of the daily bath. Indians normally bathe early in the morning for both ritual and health reasons, as well as during the day, and the British brought the habit home with them, to make cleanliness for the Westerner almost a neurosis. Up to that time bathing in the West was a rarity.

Another Indian custom adapted by the British was that of wearing the pajama, which in India is a loose-fitting, lightweight, cool trousers; by adding a top the British turned the Bengali pajama into standard attire for the night. They brought home the engaging small building known as the bungalow (a Bengali house), with its verandah or porch; named their rowboats *dinghis* after the Hindi term; and on duty wore khaki or dust-colored cloth, again from the Hindi. Calico, the cheeroot (a cigar) and the custom of the shampoo were other innovations for the English. But these are all minor. England was in India solely to make money, and this is what Englishmen as individuals, and the Company and the Government took out of India from the time of the American Revolu-

tion to the recent past. Indian money financed a large part of the British economy, and it would be an interesting but unverifiable project to speculate what would have happened to Britain without the nearly inexhaustible treasure house that was Bengal and British India.

Over a century after the height of British rule in India, it is difficult to see what made the British so arrogant toward India and her people and to their other colonies, and so confident in their own divine mission. A few quotations from various English writers of the past century clearly underline the unvarying attitude toward the Native. One administrator thought "the progress of enlightenment had been too slow," and said that progress was being resisted because "the

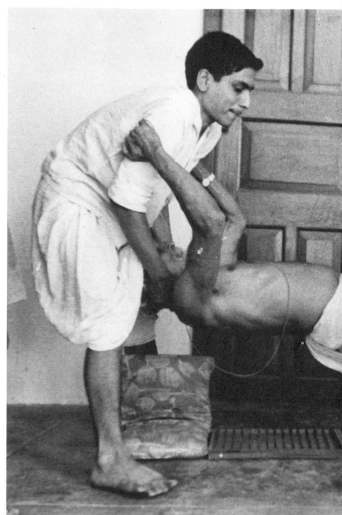

A popular manifestation of Hindu religious expression is the reading of the Bhagavad Gita, *the most popular of all the classics. Here, at an ashram in old Delhi, a priest chants the sacred text in Sanskrit, in a nonstop reading of the book.*

Not all yogis are religious men. This yogi who is being lowered to a bed of nails has spent his life learning control of his body. He can stop his pulse and his heart, has been buried in the ground for as long as a month, and lets cars and trucks run over his body, without harm.

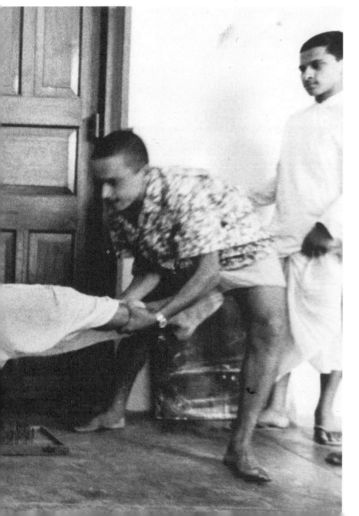

Brahmin priesthood was being threatened." (The writer wanted them eliminated.) Of Brahminic teachings he said: "Reason demonstrated their absurdity." A missionary wrote: "It is impossible to calculate the saving of human life which has resulted from the British conquest . . . . If we take the country and its people for our beloved Queen, shall we not put both it and them under the protection of the same true God?" A British historian wrote: "The worst that can be alleged against our rule is that we had with the best intentions made many mistakes, which intensified the force of the disturbances occasioned by the Mutiny [and] offended the tyrannical few, much of it . . . aroused by that resolute assertion of the majesty of the law which is the first duty of every government."

In general, the British found the people they have subjugated to be "evil-minded, designing men," "wily Asiatic intriguers," men of "degrading superstitions," and so on; it being the duty, the divine obligation of the Englishman (even those absorbed in looting India) "to hew down this dense jungle of Hindooism" and "to emanicipate the natives of India from the gross superstitions which enchained them." "It was plain to the comprehension of the guardians of Eastern learning, that what had been done to unlock the floodgates of the West, would soon appear to be as nothing in comparison with the great tide of European civilization which was about to be poured out upon them." In short, that everything that the Indians held dear and cherished, their families, customs, culture, traditions,

Meditation before the Ganges: all knowledge is contained in the river, and upon contemplation of her waters, one gains wisdom.

religion, every aspect of their life, was under attack by the English in a manner no other invader had ever attempted. Nothing was being spared, nothing was sacred to the foreigners; a revolt was inevitable.

At home the English knew very little of what was actually happening in India, and even if they had been told the details, it would have been hard to interpret them in the proper perspective and to have acted sensibly. Everyone believed that the natives were chaotic and lazy. The English governor-general who ruled from 1848 to 1856, Lord Dalhousie, had, from his point of view, the admirable aim of ending the confusion, and drew up a program for modernizing India. Local "anarchy" (it was not anarchy by Indian standards) was to be ended, and India would be able to take her place among the civilized nations of the world. Dalhousie created all-India departments to deal with civil engineering works, railways, and telegraphs and the post. His guiding principles were based on the best business practices of the West: uniformity of management and uniformity of authority. The chaos of the remaining native states was to end, as native rule was anachronistic. The princely states were steadily brought under British control.

At first Dalhousie used his powers to annex states in which there was no direct heir, rejecting the ancient Hindu custom that a childless ruler had the right to adopt an heir. This was a right exercised in any Indian family of any class or caste. On a lesser level, he annexed estates whose owners, the English felt, did not have proper title to their land. In south India alone some 20,000 estates were thus seized by the British Government. After annexing a number of minor states, Dalhousie then moved against the King of Oudh, who was the adopted son of the previous ruler, and a poor, vicious raja who misgoverned his people. Indians could see that the English were interfering with their lives on every level, from religious and social customs, to education, to all aspects of their government.

A messenger comes to the headman of a village and brings him six pancakes—chapatties, such as the Natives make of wheaten flour—and he says, "These six pancakes are sent to you—distribute them among as many villages, and make six others, and send them on with the same message to another headman." The headman obeys, accepts the six cakes, makes six others, and sends them on to the headman of the next village with the same message. . . . How did it begin? It is a mystery.

I allude to the circumstance of the lotus flower. A man came with a lotus flower and gave it to the chief soldier of a regiment. It was circulated from hand to hand in the regiment, and every man who took it looked at it and passed it on, saying nothing. We must understand that every man who passed it on was acquainted with the plot. When it came to the last soldier of the regiment he disappeared and took it to the next station. The process was gone through with every regiment in

Bengal. There was not a regiment, not a station, not an escort, among which the lotus flower has not in this way been circulated.

These two incidents are famous in the legends of the Sepoy Mutiny of 1857 and were even mentioned by the great British statesman Benjamin Disraeli (I have quoted the stories as he told them), who was the spokesman for the Opposition in the British House of Commons when England was aroused by the unexpected revolt. Delhi had been occupied, and Disraeli wanted to know the causes for the uprising. "Is it a military mutiny, or is it a national revolt?" he asked.

This was the burning question. Disraeli expressed the opinion that "the Bengal army in revolting against our authority . . . were not so much the avengers of professional grievances as the exponents of general discontent." Disraeli pays respect to British heroism: "The conquest of a country inhabited by 150,000,000 of men, in many instances of warlike habits, could at no time have been an easy achievement. . . . The annals of our warfare in India have been glorious." Disraeli accepts the cynically naive notion that England was in India because she had been frequently called upon to protect the religion and property of "populations suffering under tyranny." But in recent years, Disraeli notes, "Everything in India has been changed. Laws and manners, customs and usages, political organization, the tenure of property, the religion of the people—everything in India has either been changed or attempted to be changed, or there is a suspicion among the population that a desire for change exists on the part of our government." This, Disraeli says, has led to serious discontent. British rule has meant "our forcible destruction of native authority; next, our disturbance of the settlement of property; and thirdly, our tampering with the religion of the people." Disraeli describes these situations in detail, noting how British rule in every case has attacked cherished Indian institutions, beliefs and customs.

The annexation of Oudh, or Oude, which took place the previous year, 1856, seemed to summarize all that was wrong with British rule. The British had objected to the ruling prince, who was something of a despot, but still the legitimate ruler according to Indian belief. However the British expelled him. "The moment the throne of Oude was declared vacant, the English troops poured in; the royal treasury was ransacked, and the furniture and jewelry of the King and his wives were seized. From that instant the Mahomedan princes were all alienated. For the first time the Mahomedan princes felt that they had an identity of interest with the Hindoo Rajahs." Princes all over India realized that they were not safe from the British. Unfortunately for the Government, the bulk of the soldiers—the sepoys—in the Bengal army were subjects of the King of Oudh, some 70,000 men, according to Disraeli's information. The Oudh sepoy (the proper spelling is Oudh and not Oude as Disraeli had it), who went off as a soldier of fortune to serve under the British, now found that his homeland was a British possession, and that he was subject to all the harshness of foreign rule and had lost the protection of his prince.

The Mutiny began simply enough. In the spring of 1857 the British introduced a new type of rifle, the cartridge for which was rammed down the barrel. The cartridge was greased, and it had to be bitten by the soldier so that the powder would flow freely. It was rumored among the troops that the grease was made either of cow fat or pork fat. Since the troops of the Bengal Army, the largest of the three forces of the East India Company, were either Hindu, who did not eat meat and to whom the cow was a sacred animal, or Muslims, to whom the pig was a forbidden and unclean animal, the entire army was offended and angered by this callous disregard for their cherished religious beliefs. They refused to use the new cartridges. The British failed to see that these prejudices were important and insisted on the use of the cartridges.

A revolt suddenly broke out in the garrison at Meerut, an important small town high in the Doab, about halfway between the Ganges and the Jumna. The sepoys killed their officers, who were British, and marched on Delhi, which was forty miles to the south, capturing the city easily. Here they installed Bahadur Shah as emperor of the newly revived Moghul empire. Bahadur Shah has been described as a "helpless old man of eighty-two." There was a brief period of shock as the news of the revolt spread among both the British and the Indians, and then the rebellion seized the spirit of the people. In a matter of days the Gangetic plain from one end to the other was in revolt, claiming the loyalties not only of the troops, but of kings, nobles, princes, businessmen, and the working people and the farmers. The kingdom of Oudh, the most recent example of British imperialism at its worst, was the scene of intense fighting. The sepoys, aided by civilians, captured Lucknow, the former capital of Oudh, and Kanpur, a city on the Ganges. Other posts fell sooner or later. The British, heavily outnumbered, fought bravely and intelligently, and the battles in defense of their conquered empire filled their history books for almost a century as examples of the white man's courage in the face of native infidelity.

These accounts are too numerous to quote at length, but a typical one (by a missionary) complains "that there never was anything like affection or loyal attachment, in any true sense of the terms, on the part of the native population towards the British power, is what no one who knows them could honestly aver." The author quotes a land-holding Englishman who wrote him: "I have lost all my property; but my principle object is to impress upon my countrymen . . . the utter and most virulent hatred the natives have evinced throughout this outbreak, both to our Government and Europeans generally." The newspapers in England and those in India (which were British owned) were filled with gruesome reports of the murder of children and the rape of women. While many of these stories were obviously false (though in calmer days they weren't retracted or disproved), they served to arouse the British and to confirm them in the accepted attitudes that the natives were "murderous," of "darkened intelligence," "evil-minded, designing men," and so on. There were some Indian atrocities, notably one at Kanpur where the handful of civilians attached to the garrison, including the children, were massacred and their bodies thrown into a well. This particular incident remained for a long time to the British the symbol of the Mutiny; recently it has been de-emphasized and is now fading away in the perspective of history.

But the Mutiny could not last. Though the British saw elements of a conspiracy because of the incidents of the chapattis and the lotus, the Mutiny seemed to be more spontaneous than planned. A few natural leaders appeared who *might* have been plotting for a future rebellion. One was known as the Maulavi, who was a kind of Muslim religious leader. One of the British who opposed him said that the Maulavi, Ahmad-ullah, was "a man of great abilities, of undaunted courage, of stern determination, and by far the best soldier among the rebels." The Maulavi is credited with being the man behind the chapatti scheme, and is the one who realized the implications of the new cartridges when he was visiting sepoys at the British arsenal outside of Calcutta. Another leader was the deposed Peshwa of Oudh, Nana Sahib. A member

of the East India Company, G.B. Malleson, who tried to put the Mutiny into perspective and is one of the few foreigners to see it as the end of a long-planned rebellion, tried to explain to his countrymen that while deposing Nana Sahib "was just according to Western ideas . . . the oriental mind does not admit of the validity of an agreement which deprives a man of his kingdom and makes no provision for his family after death. Such was the grievance of Nana Sahib. He had no title in [British] law. But the natives of India believed then, they believe still, that he had a moral claim superior to all [British] law."

The third leader, according to Malleson, was the Rani of Jhansi, a small state south of Oudh, who was a gifted, energetic woman "of high character." Like Nana Sahib, she too was deprived of her kingdom by Lord Dalhousie when her husband died in 1854. "With a stroke of his pen he deprived this high-spirited woman of the rights which she believed, and which all the natives of India believed, to be hereditary." Dalhousie's greed turned the Rani "into a veritable tigress." Thus the leaders were people who had legitimate claims to fight for their rights, and throughout the century, and even to the present, the British were unable to see why the Indians resented their rule and were unable to tolerate it.

Scenes from the Mutiny: (top) a British civilian "liberates" Indians of their jewels. (Bottom) Sikhs who had fought against the British are tied to the mouths of cannons to be executed.

The fighting raged across the plain for months. The British, with better organization, better communications, heavier and more modern weapons, and aided by troops from other parts of India, finally gained control, pursuing the rebels with the utmost savagery. Delhi was retaken from the rebels in September, and six months later the British drove the sepoys out of Lucknow and Kanpur.

But it took until the end of 1858 before the last pockets of resistance were overcome, the enemy either being killed on the spot or being held for summary trials and execution. The most common method was to tie the sepoy to the mouth of a cannon and to blow him to pieces. The British troops, and indeed the public at home, were reported "maddened" by the acts of the rebels, and this served to mitigate what was to happen when the sepoys were captured. When the mutiny broke out at Lahore, the commanding officer, Major Spencer, was killed, but the civil agent, Mr. Frederick Cooper, Deputy-Commissioner of Amritsar, was able to disarm the rebels, some 3,800 sepoys, with the aid of 400 British troops and some "loyal" Sikhs; for several months the sepoys were confined to their camp. However, a break came one day, and 500 of the mutineers tried to escape by crossing a river. They were calmly shot down by the British and their allies. Cooper finally rounded up all the escapees who were alive, and after a lot of talk of "loyalty" and "betrayal," began to have them shot in groups of ten. In the book he wrote later as a kind of manual of how to keep natives in line, he remarks that there was one great "difficulty which was of sanitary consideration—the disposal of the corpses of the dishonoured soldiers." The killing went on, though one of the Sikhs, an old man, fainted from the demands on his sense of justice. Cooper made it clear to the weak-kneed reader at home:

A single Anglo-Saxon, supported by a section of Asiatics undertaking so tremendous a responsibility, and coldly presiding over so memorable an execution, without the excitement of battle, or a sense of individual injury, [was able] to imbue the proceedings [without] the faintest hue of vindictiveness. The Governors of the Punjab are of the true English stamp and mould, and knew that England expected every man to do his duty, and that duty done, thanks them warmly for it.

Cooper earned the congratulations of his peers, the British rulers of India, one, for example, writing, "I congratulate you on your success against the 26th N.I." Another, who was deeply involved in attempting to convert the Hindus to Anglicanism, wrote, "All honour for what you have done; and right well you have done it. . . . It was not policy, or soldiers, or officers, that saved the Indian Empire to England, and saved England to India. The Lord our God, He it was." For the British, as still another official wrote, "The sacrifice of five hundred villainous lives for the murder of two English is a retribution that will be remembered." And the standard account of the Mutiny, written at a later date by Sir George W.

Forrest, when the white man could take an objective view, ignores Cooper's executions and any other British "excesses" and concludes, "Justice was done, mercy shown to all who were not guilty of deliberate murder, the land cleansed of blood."

The Mutiny marks a watershed in English-Indian relations. One world was ending, and a new one, still undefined, was beginning. The Mutiny became almost an obsession with certain Englishmen: what caused it, why were the natives disloyal, and how could future mutinies be avoided. There was no one cause, no one analysis, and no one answer. The British variously ascribed the Mutiny to such causes as lack of discipline among the troops, failure to convert India to Christianity, the vagaries of the native mind, and to Russian and Persian agents. But Karl Marx, in a series of articles written for *The New York Daily Tribune* the summer of the Mutiny, says that what the British considered "a military mutiny is in truth a national revolt," pointing out that "Mussulmans and Hindus, renouncing their mutual antipathies, have combined against their common masters."

An English writer who showed some understanding of the Indian point of view feared that "Already it looks too much like a general war of white man against black." Indians, who did not begin to write about the Mutiny until later, began to consider it their first war of independence. But there is no clear-cut line. The most common reason for the Indian to rebel was the desire to remain Indian, to retain religion, customs, institutions, rulers, to be free of Westernizing influences; while for the British, there was the desire to "modernize" India, to turn it into a Westernized, Christian, industrial nation which would be easily malleable for their own purposes. But through sheer obstinacy, India refused to collaborate in this headlong rush into the modern world. However, a number of Indians were able to reflect on the events of 1857, and they saw that the British were vulnerable and that certain corollary themes the British were introducing would also help India. A true movement for independence began, and the same men the British were training and educating for subordinate roles in the Empire saw that this newfound knowledge would help them free India from the British. The Almighty may have saved India for England, but it was only to return it to the Indians at the proper time. Just ninety years after the Mutiny, India became independent.

Thuggees, worshippers of the goddess Kalai who committed ritual murders in her honor, parade at night. The British outlawed the sect and eventually it disappeared.

Going Downstream

Benares
The Bihar Famine
Patna

The first time I arrived at Benares was late at night. I had come by train, after a long trip along the Ganges. The station was wild; apparently there had been a huge meeting of holy men in the city, and now they were returning home, hundreds and hundreds of them, nearly naked, with faces and bodies painted white or ochre, carrying the three-pointed staff of Shiva, their long hair and beards matted and unkempt. They swarmed all over the train in a minute. I got my baggage out from under the crush and found a taxi for a hotel.

If there is any one city I would recommend to the tourist as typically "Indian," it is Benares. I have been there four times, and, frankly, my feeling about it is mixed. It is picturesque, chaotic, authentic, dirty, smelly, beautiful, serene, vulgar, saintly and crime-ridden. Benares is the yearly goal of hundreds of thousands of pilgrims, most of them Hindus; and of tens of thousands of tourists, who stay one night, see the Ganges at dawn and the local raja's palace at ten, the spots sacred to Buddha after lunch, and are then packed off to Delhi or Katmandu. There are also an unknown number of wandering Westerners who come through in search of holiness or drugs, since both are available, and stay a few days or a few months or years. Benares is all of India—heart, soul, body. What makes India lovable is here, and the qualities that turn one away are also here.

Benares—the Indian name the government uses is Varanasi—is said to be the world's oldest city. It was known in the past as Kashi, "that which illumines," and is called the "resplendent city of Shiva." The god's most sacred temples and shrines are here. In the symbolic microcosm of the universe as a human body, Kashi is the head, where knowledge dwells, and thus is the center of Hindu studies. In this microcosm, the three mystical arteries, the Ida, Pingala and Sushumna unite. They correspond to the three forms of the Ganges. Similarly, the earthly Kashi is at a point where the three Ganges come together: the visible river, the celestial Ganges (the Milky Way) and the subterranean stream known as the Patala Ganges or the Underworld Ganges, which is said to flow under the surface of the land directly from the Himalayas. In the five main Shiva temples of old Benares the five elements—water, earth, ether, air and fire—are worshipped.

Benares lies on the banks of the Ganges. The river has thus far headed in a southeasterly direction, but some miles west of Benares it takes a sudden twist to the north, so that what would be the upper or northern bank, is, geographically now the western bank. Almost the entire city is jammed together on this bank. The opposite bank is virtually bare, and is hardly more than a flat, sandy plain that stretches for miles eastward with little in sight but a few bamboo shacks and a railway bridge leading to the central terminal located at Mughal Sarai. On the north bank, which is steep and high, are buildings piled atop each other: palaces, slums, temples, shrines, beautiful old houses, shops, offices, monasteries and pilgrim rest houses. There are uncounted layers of civilization under today's city, accumulated because the north bank is sacred, and Indians cherish the sacred, no matter what inconvenience they must endure. Invariably the tourist asks, "Why don't you move to the other side? It's empty." And the answer is, "But it is not sacred!"

Benares is to the Indian the rough equivalent of Rome to the Christian, with an intensity and transcendence which Rome may have had but has lost. Rome has always been, firstly, a secular city. Benares is sacred beyond measure; it is a mystical experience and the pilgrim is transfixed as he bathes in the Ganges or makes the thirty-four mile long walk along Panchkosi Road. The day is an endless ritual of washing and prayer. The most propitious moment is at sunrise, when the sun punches a hole in the gray-blue screen to the east, and then in a matter of minutes overwhelms the city in its brilliance and heat. Because of the angle of the earth's axis, the tropics have an almost continual high noon; there is no slow awakening and long decline as northern people know the day. In India the sun drops suddenly, and there is a dark that is blacker than that of the north, because fewer stars are seen in the tropics. As the sun retreats from the white-hot sky and becomes almost visible colonies of widows come down to the banks of the river. They have already bathed several times during the day, but they bathe again. They are fully clothed in white mourn-ing saris and immerse themselves as they are, and then stand on the stone steps of the bank, to change their six yards of wet, clinging sari without exposing themselves.

And then, all is dark. Most people stay at home, although there are a few night spots, some restaurants and movie houses. The evening silence is broken only by the sound of temple bells and conch shells.

It seems like a sacrilege, but the oldest city in the world is about to be modernized. I am seated in a bungalow on the outskirts of the city in the offices of the regional planning commission.

"The big problem up to now is that Benares did not have a stable economic base," a round-faced little man named Singh tells me. The economy has survived on the pilgrim trade, but now the city is to be industrialized. There is already a big diesel locomotive works in a suburb, and the largest rail center in India, at Mughal Sarai, is across the Ganges. Indians are proud of their railways, and I must say that I am impressed by their trains, which are well kept and as on schedule as those few remaining relics in my own country. A lot of the future development, Mr. Singh says, will take place along the railway. The present industry is minor. There is an excellent toy industry, which the local people are ashamed of—they are gradually replacing their charming traditional toys—animals and birds carved of wood and brightly painted, and kites and little carts and noise-makers—with direct copies of Western toys. A Mr. Aguilar takes me to a village outside Benares where the people have traditionally made toys, and tells me he wants them to change to items for the American market. He shows me a few ghastly samples he has made. "Don't you think they will sell?" he asks hopefully. I tell him No, he should export Indian toys to America because they are so beautiful, charming and well made, but he is not impressed.

Benares is also famous for its silks, most of which are cut into saris (a sari is six yards long). This silk is finely woven and has gold or silver thread forming intricate patterns. Among the local people these are known as Tourist Saris, because these are what the foreign visitor brings home as a typical Indian sari most likely to be cut up into dresses. Only the most wealthy Indian woman would wear such a sari, and then only on special occasions. The rickshaw drivers take their foreign riders to the tiny shops where the saris are sold; usually there are looms in the back with weavers swiftly shooting the shuttles back and forth with incredible dexterity. They receive a few cents a day, but the finished sari will sell for thirty to a hundred dollars. One of my drivers, despite my protests, brings me to a large central shop run by the state of Uttar Pradesh. It is full of Americans on tour. A salesman urges everyone to sit on the floor on large mats covered with white sheets. This is the normal way of doing business in shops in India. The Americans reluc-

A toymaker at a village near Benares. Indian toys follow traditional patterns and styles, some of which go back four thousand years.

tantly sit down, though a few stand at the back, and there are some chairs for the culturally awkward. A few assistants deftly unroll saris; suddenly there is a great profusion of silks in bright colors, pinks, soft greens and peacock blues, and deep purples, and chocolate browns, all laced and adorned and threaded with intricate golds and silvers. The effect is magnificent: this is regal India spread out before the pale, sweating barbarians. The salesman urges a woman to come forward. A slim woman in a wash-and-wear dress, her hair tinted and teased and lacquered, comes forward awkwardly, and the salesman quickly drapes the sari around her. Suddenly *she* is a Moghul princess, graceful and commanding. Another woman is decorated. The Americans have been conquered. Traveler's checks come out, the saris are wrapped, there are bows and *namaskars,* and the tourists get back into the limousines.

The saris are amazingly fine; they fold down to a slim package about twelve by fifteen inches by a half inch thick, but unfolded they will be eighteen feet long by forty-five to forty-eight inches. I wonder what these women will do when they are confronted with the mystery of these shimmering yards of cloth, because tying the sari is a mysterious skill that an Indian woman is born with, just as she is born with liquid enigmatic eyes and skin like tawny satin and the movements of a black panther.

"You buy sari for wife," my rickshawallah says. "Wife has sari," I snap at him. His name is Govind, and he is a human wreck. He has attached himself to me. It is a kind of feudal relationship, and in my early days in India I was uncomfortable. I cannot use another driver, much as I would like to. Govind moves at half the pace of the other rickshawallahs, as if he were in a dream. At first I would urge him to go faster, but then I accepted reality. He was continually stoned: he chewed raw betel nut, which is a crude narcotic, and then opium; he smoked *ganja,* which is the Indian term for marijuana. I used to buy him food— I would get him bunches of bananas, and crackers, and take him to a stall for bowls of rice and curried vegetables, just to keep him from collapsing. I overpaid him outrageously, that is, giving him forty cents for a day's work, when the going price was twenty for a knowledgeable Westerner and ten for an Indian. But Govind was reliable. I learned to allow an extra half hour or hour for our trips—I was wandering all over Benares, and to Sarnath, the Buddhist sanctuary five miles outside the city. He was always waiting for me, and if I wanted an early start he would sleep in the rickshaw outside the bungalow where I stayed, with nothing against the cold (it was the beginning of winter) except a worn cotton shirt and a mouthful of betel nut and opium. And when I would stagger out into the early morning mist to go down to the river (the part I liked to visit was a good three miles away), he would jump to his feet and say, "Hey, Boss, this way," while the other rickshawallahs clamored for my business, knowing, however, that I would have to go with Govind.

Mr. Singh tells me that besides the minor industries like toys and saris, Benares will soon have factories for tractors and other heavy equipment. The problem is a paucity of raw materials. "And then there is population," he adds. "The present population is 5.8 lakhs. It will reach sixteen lakhs by 1991. We have estimated forty-five percent growth per decade. Reason is huge birthrate despite family planning, migration to the city for jobs though there are no jobs. We will have to build new housing. Two lakhs of new units are proposed by 1991. But none are started yet." A lakh is 100,000, and my mind is getting confused trying to put the number into Western figures.

Benares now has a population of 580,000 people, which will almost triple by 1991, when it will have an estimated 1,600,000 people. The figures are overwhelming, and the problems seem insoluble, but Indians are invariably optimistic. There are huge maps on the wall, showing Benares at different stages, when it was Kashi and a small holy city, and then through various stages of growth. Different areas are marked off in colors. Mr. Singh points at the maps with a long stick, which keeps going off the edge of the paper or into a different area as if it had a mind of its own (not an uncommon phenomenon in India) and wanted to poke holes in his talk.

I close my notebook and thank Mr. Singh. He smiles expansively because he knows I am working on an article on urban development in India and he has been extremely helpful. Govind has

been waiting at a betel nut stand across the road. He looks no more stoned than usual, and we set off at his dreamlike pace, his bare feet hard on the metal of the pedals (the rubber plugs have long since worn away). On the side of the road a small blind man is curled up over a drum made of an inverted coffee tin; his fingers move over the edge and the metal skin, finding tones and sounds that go back to the days of Kashi and the heavenly Buddha.

Dusk. Most of the pilgrims have finished bathing, and now women are performing another ritual. They light a tiny candle and place it on a large leaf, which is floated away on the surface of the river. Someone gives me a candle and a leaf, and I follow the ritual. A man

rule is "severe." He had a highly organized, efficient bureaucracy, a high tax structure (up to a third of a man's income, leaving the peasants normally destitute each year), a law-and-order legislative system fed by a terroristic secret police. The *Arthashastra*, a treatise written by a Magadha court philosopher on how to get ahead in life, listed eighteen kinds of torture which might be used by the state to keep people in line; the death penalty was freely bestowed, in a variety of brutal ways. Magadha was further expanded with the emperor's son.

Meanwhile, the Gautama Buddha was born in a small town not far from Pataliputra. At the age of twenty-eight he abandoned his family (he was a minor prince) and went into the jungle to seek salvation. The next year, while sitting under a great, aged tree, he experienced a flash of enlightenment. After a period of further meditation, he emerged from seclusion with a new, middle-of-the-road doctrine which rejected the formalism and ritual of the Hindu priesthood and the severe asceticism of many holy men and offered salvation to every man if he would work for it. Buddhism had a great appeal to the masses, who were denied the privileges of the higher-caste Hindu priests, and it soon challenged the religious establishment with its message of equality, peace and brotherhood. In 261 B.C., Asoka, the grandson of Chandragupta, experienced an unusual and sudden conversion to Buddhism. Asoka had just concluded a very bloody war against other Indian states, in which hundreds of thousands of people fell victim to his soldiers. The cruelty, wastefulness and sin of war overwhelmed him at the very moment when he was riding in victory with his entourage through the ruins of an enemy city. Asoka drew up a series of edicts which were carved on pillars and placed throughout the empire proclaiming the primacy of peace and the subjection of the ruler to his people as their servant. Few leaders in history have experienced such a sudden change of mind, and none has made such an effort to put this kind of strict moral decision into practice. Asoka did not force Buddhism upon India, which might have brought a violent reaction in people who still adhered to Hinduism, but he did follow Buddhist principles of non-violence and brotherhood. However, his successors lacked his qualities of leadership, and in 185 B.C. the barbarians coming over the western mountain passes lopped off substantial portions of outlying Magadha.

The empire saw a great revival in the fourth century A.D. In A.D. 320 a warrior prince from the same tribal family into which Buddha had been born took over the state of Magadha, by this time a rambling provincial outpost, and turned

The spot at Sarnath (near Benares) where Buddha gave his first sermon. A monastery was later built on the site, but subsequently was abandoned when Buddhism died out in India. Now the government has excavated the site.

it into a new Indian superstate, which, within a few decades, ranged from Bengal across the Gangetic plain to the upper sections of the Doab. This revived empire, under the Gupta dynasty, was not only a military but an economic, cultural and religious success. India has from this period a wealth of artistic works—cave paintings, temples, literary, philosophical, and scientific works. The poet, Kalidasa, known as the Indian Shakespeare, lived under the Guptas. Two of his major works, *Sakuntala*, a play, and *The Cloud Messenger*, a long poem, were translated from Sanskrit into English in the late eighteenth century, capturing the minds and imagination of European Romantics, among them Goethe.

Ordinary commercial techniques were highly developed. There is, for example, an iron pillar, now outside of Delhi, which is of such purity and fineness that it is rustproof, being smelted by methods that were rediscovered only recently. There was steady trade with the West, accompanied by an exchange of knowledge, which included the West's discovery that the Indians had a system of mathematics superior to theirs. Indian traders and missionaries went deep into southeast Asia and the offshore islands, colonizing Indochina and Indonesia. Indian life was on a higher plane than that of Europe, which at the time was experiencing a long age of decline, the Dark Ages, when barbarians were overrunning the fading Roman empire and destroying a thousand years of Western civilization. But throughout the Guptas' empire, life was at a new level. An Indian document from Benares describes what life was like for the man of leisure, that is, the man with lands and a private income, who has no other role in life but to enjoy himself in the company of friends.

He should take a house in a city, or large village, or in the vicinity of good men, or in a place which is the resort of many persons. This abode should be situated near some water, and divided into different compartments for different purposes. It should be surrounded by a garden, and also contain two rooms, an outer and an inner one. The inner room should be occupied by the females, while the outer room, balmy with rich perfumes, should contain a bed, soft, agreeable to the sight, covered with a clean white cloth, low in the middle part, having garlands and bunches of flowers upon it, and a canopy above it, and two pillows, one at the top, another at the bottom. There should be also a sort of couch besides, and at the head of this a sort of stool, on which should be placed the fragrant ointments for the night, as well as flowers, pots containing collyrium and other fragrant substances, things used for perfuming the mouth, and the bark of the common citron tree. Near the couch, on the ground, there should be a pot for spitting, a box containing ornaments, and also a lute hanging from a peg made of the tooth of

Untouchables in a Bihar village. They are chamars, or leatherworkers. Because they handle the bodies of animals they are outside the caste system of orthodox Hinduism. Note the effects of malnutrition on the boy.

While the local inhabitants carry on their work at the well, homeless people who come to Bihar for relief food sit on the ground waiting for some change in their lives.

In a good season the plain is rich with fat cattle walking through lush green fields.

an elephant, a board for drawing, a pot containing perfume, some books, and some garlands of the yellow amaranth flowers. Not far from the couch, and on the ground, there should be a round seat, a toy cart, and a board for playing with dice; outside the outer room there should be cages of birds, and a separate place for spinning, carving and such like diversions. In the garden there should be a whirling swing and a common swing, and also a bower of creepers covered with flowers, in which a raised parterre should be made for sitting.

Now the householder, having got up in the morning and performed the necessary duties, should wash his teeth, apply a limited quantity of ointments and perfumes to his body, put some ornaments

on his person and collyrium on his eyelids and below his eyes, colour his lips with alacktaka, and look at himself in the glass. Having then eaten betel leaves, with other things that give fragrance to the mouth, he should perform his usual business. He should bathe daily, anoint his body with oil every other day, apply a lathering substance to his body every three days, get his head (including face) shaved every four days and the other parts of his body every five or ten days. All these things should be done without fail, and the sweat of the armpits should also be removed. Meals should be taken in the forenoon, in the afternoon, and again at night. After breakfast, parrots and other birds should be taught to speak, and the fighting of cocks, quails, and rams should

follow. A limited time should be devoted to diversions [with friends], and then the midday sleep should be taken. After this the householder, having put on his clothes and ornaments, should, during the afternoon, converse with his friends. In the evening there should be singing, and after that the householder, along with his friend, should await in his room, previously decorated, the arrival of the woman that may be attached to him, or he may send a female messenger for her, or go for her himself. After her arrival at his house, he and his friend should welcome her, and entertain her with a loving and agreeable conversation. Thus ends the duties of the day.

The author suggests other occasional pastimes, such as "Holding festivals in honor of different Deities," "social gatherings of both sexes," "drinking parties," "picnics," and "bathing in summer in water from which wicked or dangerous animals have previously been taken out, and which has been built in on all sides."

There may be some people who live like that today in Patna, but if they do, they keep it quiet. A few of the maharajahs tried to continue such a life after Independence in 1947, but the confiscation of their states, jewels, palaces, and the levying of impossible taxes have reduced most of them to middle-class stature. When I was in Patna the character of the city gave no clue to its imperial past. Student revolutionaries had just burned down a government-sponsored cottage industry warehouse, and the city was in turmoil. The famine was still devastating the countryside, and Patna was flooded with refugees begging for food. Gupta India had long since disappeared. Patna's subsequent history after the Guptas is rather confusing and boring. The dynasty declined, as all dynasties do, and then the Muslims ranged back and forth across the area. "Blood and business" are the words one English writer applies to the city, for Dutch merchants arrived at the end of the sixteenth century, primarily for the area's two great crops, opium and indigo, the latter being a blue dye. Musk from the Himalayas, drugs from China, lac (the basic ingredient in lacquer) and taffeta were other important items of trade. In 1620 two Englishmen named Hughes and Parker came down from Agra to buy cloth. By 1657 the English were able to get a foothold in the saltpeter business, the chemical then being an important ingredient in gunpowder. Large quantities of saltpeter were shipped downstream to Calcutta. Meanwhile, minor wars among the natives swirled around the English merchants. But in 1680 the saltpeter factory was taken over by Emperor Aurangzeb, and the trade was stopped and a heavy tax imposed on all foreign trading. There then followed a confused time of social turmoil, with attacks by Afghans and Marathas, revolts and palace conspiracies, and full-scale occupation by the English, who seemed to be endlessly installing puppet governors and then deposing them.

Whatever dispute arose, the East India

A well-to-do Brahmin family. They control their village, and are better educated than the lower-caste peasants who work for them.

Company was favored. For example, when a man named Mir Jafar was installed as Nawab of Bengal at Patna in 1757 after a period of fluctuating battles, the British demanded an enormous compensation for the "losses" suffered during the fighting. The Company wanted ten million rupees for itself, five million for members of the English colony, two million for various pro-British Indians, one million for the Armenians who held certain interests and another five million for the Crown's Army and Navy, which had been of use to the Company. Various individuals also demanded sums of hundreds of thousands of rupees. Clive's claim totaled 640,000 alone. "The English still cherished extravagant ideas of Indian wealth," wrote an official British historian in 1886. "But no funds existed to satisfy their inordinate demands, and they had to be content with one-half the stipulated sums. Even of this reduced amount, one-third had to be taken in jewels and plate, there being neither coin nor bullion left."

What probably reduced Patna to its present role as a provincial backwater was the decline of the opium trade. The British put in a railway to link Patna to other key cities, and the roads and river traffic were developed. Better access to new markets led the farmers to change to other crops which could be easier grown and harvested, and which would

bring a quicker return than opium, which required a lot of work, from planting, growing, tapping the milk, and processing it into a saleable product. Opium production, as a major industry, gradually faded away. It was economics rather than morality that killed opium as a source of revenue for Company and Crown.

Another train ride along the river. It is a third-class car, a local train from a town called Dehri-on-Son. The car is filled with peasants going to market with baskets of vegetables, a goat, chickens. The women sit on the floor with their heads covered because there is a foreigner present. The compartment is so crowded that the people hang outside the door, but every time we come to a station more people clamber into it. A husky young farmer sitting next to me asks me where I have come from. "American aid is being wasted," he says. "All you do is keep us on the starvation line. If each American who came to hand out food would take on a group of five villages and help them get on their feet we would make some progress. Show the farmers how to farm properly. Bring in the new seeds, the new fertilizers. Ten thousand Americans, 50,000 villages. In ten years India would be saved.

"The money you are putting into the relief projects in the cities is being wasted, thrown away. Help India at the source: the farms."

I am on my way to Bodh Gaya, the spot where Buddha received enlightenment. A young American couple is there; they are relief workers; the husband works for an American charity, so I tell him what the farmer told me about American relief and the plan for starting with the villages. "He's right of course," said the American. "Are you going to go to your boss and tell him?" I asked. "No," he said, and he proceeded to tell me why it wouldn't work, the main reason being that he was committed to giving away so many tons of food a year and that was precisely what they were going to do.

Another train. I am riding from Bodh Gaya to Benares, this time in the first-class carriage. The seats are a kind of black, ancient synthetic material and covered with dust. Third class, with its wooden benches, seems cleaner. A group of businessmen get into my compartment and begin chattering away in Hindi. But someone says in English, "Laxshmi, the goddess of wealth." The countryside is fertile and rich, the fields are green, but the riverbeds are completely dry. The air is clear, dry, and not too hot. This is India as the tourists want to see it: small boys sitting on great black water buffaloes, women in bright colors with gleaming brass water pots on their heads, farmers with herds of cattle crossing the fields. The sun, sinking quickly in the west, has given the sky some color. For a few minutes it is a blue-gray, and some scattered clouds turn to pinks and violets. The train rattles across a long bridge; we are crossing a river which looked like the Son. The Son is as wide as the Ganges in this area, and as erratic, but the bed is almost dry. There are some cattle drinking, and then I see a tremendous group of women filling their water pots, perhaps two or three hundred of them in an amazing blaze of color and going away in a long file with the pots balanced on their heads with the long easy swing of arms and legs and straight back that gives so much dignity and beauty to the Indian peasant woman. Suddenly the echoing changes into more solid sound of tracks on earth; we have crossed the Son and are on the plain, and darkness descends. I turn the lights on in the compartment; the businessmen have gone and now a man in a uniform is sitting opposite me. He is with a young boy. "You are coming from —?" he says. "America." He is pleased. The boy is his son, "You were staying —?" I tell him, "Calcutta." "Bengali side

A boatman offers trinkets and rosaries to pilgrims on the Ganges.

very bad," says the policeman. "Maoist people, crazy, thieves." But America— he suddenly quotes a snatch of an American patriotic poem I remember vaguely from my childhood, "This is my own, my native land—" and he lapses into Hindi, in which the poem sounds much better, more dignified, more substantial. "You have to love your own country, America, India, England."

Golden Bengal

Women pounding grain in a Hindu village in the delta. People congregate by religion and caste, and even occupation, in the villages.

As she approaches the 88th meridian, the Ganges enters the narrow northern neck of West Bengal and turns sharply south. Here the river breaks up into her Hundred Mouths. The main flow continues into East Bengal, while a smaller but most sacred offshoot, the Hooghly, drops down to Calcutta and continues another eighty miles through treacherous shallows, sandbars, twists and turns, and tidal movements into the great Bay of Bengal. At the dividing point between Indian Bengal and East Bengal, which until the end of 1971 had been East Pakistan, a barrage (a complex of dams and sluices) was being constructed in order to harness the energies of the Ganges and to help control flooding. However, the barrage had been the subject of continual disputes between India and Pakistan, and the work went slowly. The civil war that shook East Pakistan in 1971 halted construction of the barrage, and it was years before construction could be resumed.

Bengal is a country within a country. Perhaps no other area of the great subcontinent is so pronounced in its uniqueness and is as succinct a summary of "India" as is Bengal. Where the Ganges has been but a single flow for most of its journey, in Bengal it assumes a hundred shapes, like an Indian goddess with a hundred arms, eyes, mouths. Joined by other streams flowing from the Himalayas, the river deepens, broadens, wanders, gets lost, reappears, changes name, dies and is reborn.

The Bengal delta, coveniently labeled the Old Delta and the New Delta by geographers because one is simply older than the other, which is still being formed, is low, flat, rich with vegetation, swelling with life. The frightfully arid plain of Uttar Pradesh and Bihar, so desiccated and stark, suddenly gives way to an explosive burst of tropical jungle and green fields in a matter of a few miles. There are mangrove swamps everywhere, and ruined and abandoned cities, old palaces and the capitals of empires, forts and factories, mansions and plantations, pirate strongholds and counting houses, once the hope of Hindus, Muslims, Turks, Portuguese, Dutch and the English.

The southernmost border of the plain and the delta is surrounded by a higher escarpment, the Chota Nagpur Plateau, a rich area of great natural wealth that helps make West Bengal the key to India's economic success, but also contributes to many of her social problems. The plateau, towering some fifteen hundred feet above the lowlands, slopes off into the valley of the Damodar River. The entire region is saturated with coal, iron ore and limestone, which have enabled India to center its massive steel industry in this region. Vast industrial complexes have grown up on the plateau and in the Damodar Valley. There are also deposits of bauxite, mica and manganese, and the abundance of waterpower is being harnessed in great hydroelectrical plants. Railways connect the area to the port of Calcutta. Besides the heavy industry, there are chemical, cement, and light manufacturing plants. South of Calcutta on the Hooghly, a great new

Young goats are readied for sacrifice to Kali in a village in rural Bengal. Their heads will be offered to the goddess, and the bodies roasted for the low-caste people in the village.

port, Haldia, is under construction, with the twin aims of drawing off part of the city's excess population by providing both jobs and housing and of offering a quicker access to the ocean, for the section of the river between Calcutta and Haldia is slowly dying to heavy shipping. The Channel is heavily silted and suffers from the erratic tidal flows, wandering sandbars and changes of course; it is also too shallow for the new types of large ships with deeper drafts; many of them also are too lengthy to navigate the Hooghly's sharp bends.

The industrial cities and towns have drawn many men from the farms of Bengal, Bihar, Uttar Pradesh and Orissa. Labor and political unrest are constant companions to the new industrial production. Some of the farms are now seriously hampered by the shortage of males. On the lowlands the main product is rice, the eternal crop of the Ganges. Some sixty to seventy percent of the land is under cultivation in the western or old part of the delta, while in the newer section up to eighty percent of the land is cultivated. Besides rice, the eastern delta, which is the nation of Bangladesh, is heavily planted with jute, a crop that is used in the making of burlap and other similar rough fabrics. Rice and jute dominate the delta farmlands, since both are grown in wetlands. There are very few dry crops such as millet or peas, though there is some oilseed, sugar cane, cotton and tobacco. Upland in Bangladesh and in Assam, tea is the main crop.

Bangladesh is a compact area of some 200 by 300 miles. It has some highlands, and a tongue of land that lies adjacent to the Indian state of Assam and reaches Burma. Three quarters of the nation lives fifty feet or less above sea level, and so is subject not only to heavy flooding but also to tidal waves and other sea-caused disasters. During the floods the rivers and channels may often change course, creating new islands or merging old ones, or returning to former beds. There is endless litigation among the farmers over lost land or over newborn silt banks (known as *chars*), which offer the small cultivator a chance at a few more yards to till.

The eastern delta has few railways and not many roads. It is water which serves as the means of communcation — there are some 3,000 miles of riverways. Virtually everything goes by boat, from people to crops to equipment to armies. Even the ambulances from the clinics and hospitals are boats.

The delta contains two great cities: Calcutta, the second largest city in the British Commonwealth, with a population of somewhere between eight and twelve million; and Dacca, which was the capital of East Pakistan and is now the capital of the recently established nation of Bangladesh.

The delta was always the ultimate goal of the empire builders, whether Hindu, Turkish or British. In 1947 the delta was the scene of great tragedy when it was partitioned between India and Pakistan.

In the lush delta of Bangladesh, men take a bath after their day's work. In the background is a Muslim village.

The western portion which was largely Hindu went to India and the eastern, heavily Muslim, went to Pakistan. The delta had already experienced a crippling famine during World War II, when the British, in order to prevent a potential invasion from the Japanese based in Burma, destroyed masses of food. Officially a million people died of hunger and disease, but Bengalis who survived the famine say that the true figure is three million.

During Partition, when Hindus and Muslims had worked themselves to a high pitch of communal hatred and peo- ple began to flee across Bengal to sup- posed safety with co-religionists, hun- dreds of thousands of people were killed. By 1970 there were an estimated 110 million Bengalis, about seventy-five mil- lion living in East Bengal, then East Pakistan, and thirty-five million living in the Indian state of West Bengal. Pro- jections estimated that East Bengal alone, an area of 55,000 square miles, would have over 100 million people by the end of the century. West Bengal is in- creasing at the same rate. Bengal had al- ways been harshly ruled, but among the poorer people there was a great attraction

to Islam, and the Muslim rulers made large numbers of converts. About half the Bengalis were Muslim by the time of Partition. The British treated Bengal as a great treasury, looting as they wished. The eastern section was a backwater but valued for its raw jute, which was processed in the mills around Calcutta. Partition separated the jute fields from the mills, to the disadvantage of both sectors. Though the delta is a favored land for rice paddies, East Bengal had reached the point where it sold its highly-valued rice abroad and imported cheaper rice from Burma, this being the way in which the various Hindu, Muslim and British plantation owners and businessmen preferred to work.

Although both Muslim and Hindu had arisen spontaneously and jointly in their common cause against the Crown during the Sepoy Mutiny, Muslims began to agitate not only for Independence but for a separate Muslim state. The British

Their muzzles covered to keep them from eating the grain they are trodding, a team of cattle circle the threshing grounds of an East Bengal village. The farmer has the typical beard of the Indian Muslim.

Islamabad, where a new capital is being built. The West had forty percent of the population but sixty percent of the land, and was ruled by a notorious cabal known as the Twenty-two Families, who put their own people in government, refused democratic elections, and exploited East Pakistan. The standard of living was twice as high in the West as in the East; American aid to Pakistan remained in the West.

The one thing that united West and East was a belief in Islam as the Way. The West Pakistanis, as they like to point out, are taller, lighter skinned, aggressive and warlike. They speak a number of languages, the most prominent of which is Urdu, the lingua franca that developed out of Hindustani for use by the Turkish-Moghul armies and administrative forces. The Bengalis are smaller, darker, fine-boned, highly intellectual and volatile, and charming. They speak their own language, and their culture is at a high level. The Bengalis soon began to resent the West because they were denied a part in the rule of their own country even though Bengal supplied seventy percent of Pakistan's foreign exchange. But the Punjabis, as the Bengalis called their oppressors, ruled with the iron hand of the Turk and the Moghul.

encouraged this Muslim separatist movement, not because they wanted India partitioned, but because it played one Indian against another; and independence did not in truth seem a possibility, but a pastime for the "natives." When the disastrous dichotomy between Hindu and Muslim became a reality in 1947, Muslim Pakistan was split into two sections eleven hundred miles apart. The center of power was in West Pakistan, at Karachi and then at Rawalpindi-

However the western, that is Indian, portion of Bengal was hardly better off. Without the raw jute supplied by East Bengal, the Calcutta mills suffered disastrously; rice fields in the West were turned to jute but this created a shortage of food. Millions of Hindu refugees had entered over-populated West Bengal after Partition—they were crowded, undernourished, chronically ill—and the Bengalis found themselves among the poorest people of the subcontinent. The British had established their empire in Calcutta, but moved it to New Delhi in 1931, where the initial building had begun in 1913. The Bengalis resented this shift of the center of power. After Independence, the seat of government remained in New Delhi, and since then there has been a constant battle between the Centre, as it is called, and Calcutta. Meanwhile, international politics played a major note in the fate of both Pakistan and India. Both countries were desperately in need of foreign aid for development, and even to keep their people alive. America sent food, but also armaments, some $150,000,000 worth to In-

dia, and some $630,000,000 to Pakistan. What were these impoverished countries to do with these massive amounts of guns, tanks and artillery? Pakistan invaded India twice in border disputes, which were soon halted by outside pressure but without a satisfactory resolution of the problems.

Meanwhile Bengal continued to smolder. Neither part was playing its proper role in its national government. Indian Bengal supplies somewhere between thirty and forty percent of the nation's industry, foreign trade and taxes. Not much of the money returns to the state. The Bengali peasant is notoriously poor. His life is hard, and there is little future. The average farmer weighs about ninety-six pounds and his wife eighty-five, as I found out when I was doing research on a medical project there. Everyone, without exception, suffers from such chronic diseases as hookworm (100 percent among rural adults), leprosy (seven to fourteen percent), respiratory infections (one third of the children, for example), malaria, elephantiasis, malnutrition, and numerous other tropical afflictions.

Calcutta

The leprous beggars thrust their withered stumps into the tourists' taxis at the intersections; a child-mother offers her shriveled baby like a doll; weeping, she bares her decaying teeth. A crowd gathers around a sacred cow lying on the pavement in the convulsions of death. A group of men walk swiftly down the street carrying a *charpoy*—an Indian frame bed laced with rope—on which is the flower-covered body of a man; the head sways back and forth to the rhythm of the walkers. A few blocks further on, in front of the Park Street Police Station, is a big flat-bed truck on which lies the body of a policeman. Sticks of incense surround the corpse, and the truck is almost buried in flowers. The man had been killed that morning by a group of assassins, who were believed by the authorities to be members of an underground revolutionary movement. Amid the Communist slogans on the walls of a park is painted in red, "Welcome Stokely Carmichael," but the sign is fading away. The acid smell of Calcutta pervades everything; one puts on fresh clothing and the odor is still present. An American woman remarks, "Calcutta is supposed to be the worst city in the world. I think they're proud of it."

Calcutta does not go out of her way to please. But bad as she is, she is also one of the greatest cities of the world, a vast vibrating complex of broad avenues and narrow slum lanes, crumbling tenements and palaces, modern offices and Victorian Gothic, usually combined with sensual Hindu, luxury hotels and "Indian" lodging houses where one brings his own food and bedding. Visually the city is overwhelming, from the great maidan, or park, that forms the central core of the downtown area with its red sandstone and marble relics of the British, to the tiny back alley with one-man factories where you can get a pair of sandals, a motor, a sitar, a bolt of finely woven raw silk in peacock colors, incense in erotic scents, simple pyjamas, dhotis and saris of homespun khadi, the white cloth that Gandhi made a symbol of Indian independence. Everywhere are beautiful little parks with slime-green pools full of splashing children, and great mansions, crumbling and fading, protected by high walls and lush greenery from the squatters who fill every corner of the city.

The people's Calcutta is a mass of tenements, hovels, temples, mosques, shrines, warehouses, shops and factories. Over the city hangs the smoke of tens of thousands of cow dung cooking fires. On the walls, for block after block, are plastered flattened cow cakes to dry, each with a delicate abstract pattern from the fingers of the woman who picked it from the streets and squashed it into a patty. Over the Ujjala Theatre and a hundred others are giant posters painted on cloth with the plump vacant faces of nubile stars breathing heavily, their *bindis*, the red spot Indian women paint on their foreheads, blazing like setting suns. The city is full of outsiders—Bihari working men with their heads wrapped in colored cloth to stop the perspiration, country people coming with drums and flutes for festivals at the Kalighat, the most sacred spot in Calcutta. A Communist parade comes and goes, a hundred clerks protesting some injustice or other that will have to be corrected with a bomb. In New Alipore young matrons talk about children and clothes, and the difficulty of finding servants. They might as well be in Westchester or Oak Park. Their husbands work for large international companies, charitable institutions, or research projects. Some beggar children come up to me, smiling. "No momma, no poppa, give baksheesh." I reply, "Me no momma no poppa," but give them some money and they run off. Along Park Street, which is Calcutta's Fifth Avenue, the plump matrons wander from shop to shop to buy clothing or pastries; they are dressed in iridescent silk saris, expensive and just short of good taste.

Calcutta lies low, flat and muggy between river systems and salt lakes. Unlike other cities, she cannot radiate outwards because the land is too swampy for extensive urban sprawl. The Hooghly, having left Mother Ganges a hundred miles to the north, divides the city into Calcutta proper and Howrah, a vast flat slum which contains the great railway terminus that connects Bengal with the rest of India. The Hooghly flows through Calcutta in a muddy boil, carrying the topsoil of a hundred thousand farms from Uttar Pradesh and Bihar. There is one bridge across the Hooghly to the plain, something like Manhattan's having but a single bridge to link New York to Brooklyn or New Jersey. But in Calcutta and its suburbs are something like 8,000,000 people, plus the uncounted numbers that fled East Bengal after the rebellion of

1971. In its heterogenous population Calcutta resembles New York, it is a city of outsiders. The old Calcutta families number, perhaps, fifteen percent of the population. The rest of the city — workers, creative people, businessmen, entrepreneurs, clerks, beggars, servants, prostitutes — often come from other areas, either from the villages of Bengal or from neighbors like Bihar to the north, Orissa to the south, or even from as far away as Bombay, on the west coast. One can spend weeks in Calcutta without meeting a proper Calcuttan. In India ancient roots are more important than immediate ones, and I have met families from other parts of India now in their third generation in the city who still call themselves Punjabis or Rajasthanis. Other families, particularly the poor working people, exist on a near-commutation basis, particularly the Biharis. When conditions get bad in their home villages they migrate in great waves, especially at the time of harvest and famine, when supposedly more jobs are available in Calcutta. If they are lucky, the migrants may find themselves in the *bustees*, huge collections of shacks made of cardboard, tin, or woven palm fronds, where six to ten people live in a single room. The better bustees have a latrine for every ten shacks, but many lack even this convenience.

The unfortunate sleep in the streets. At night, in my wandering around the city, I would see the street sleepers lying everywhere, like so many casualties of a great battle. Sometimes they are lined up in orderly rows, but occasionally they are tossed about as if a great explosion had dumped them without plan. There are degrees of such poverty. Some people have a mat and a blanket, others one or the other, and many have nothing but the Calcutta pavement with all its slime as a bed. At the risk of sounding callous, I might comment that sleeping on the ground is not as great a hardship for a peasant family as would be for the Westerner. Many Indians sleep on the ground in their villages. Even city dwellers move to the streets on hot nights and most nights are hot. Families that are better off often sleep on the roofs of their houses or apartments on a graceful wooden frame bed, the charpoy, which can be picked up easily and stored away during the day.

The great tragedy in Calcutta is that there are so few jobs for the working man and woman, and thus the immediate problem is finding food. This is a constant struggle which takes precedent over housing. But it is depressing to know that tens of thousands of families in Calcutta never, in their entire lives, have a roof over their heads except in the most transitory sense. Families for uncounted generations have raised their children on the street. A lucky family will be able to rent a tiny stall, about five feet square, where they will keep their possessions. This gives them a legal address, in the rare case that they can get a ration card.

An old starving beggarwoman sleeps on the pavement of Calcutta's Park Street, the center of upper-class shopping.

But they sleep on the street, whole families huddled together on a few small straw mats. In the rainy season, which is highly unpleasant because of heavy flooding, they huddle in doorways, or under carts, wherever there is the slightest shelter.

Bengalis are known as the intellectuals of India. They are volatile, intense, intelligent, witty, sarcastic, energetic, neurotic. Conversation is good, particularly in Calcutta (though liberally spiced with complaints: against each other, against politicians, the cost of living, the government of Mrs. Gandhi). There is

still an active Bengali culture—drama, music, literature—though Calcuttans claim it is not like the old days. There are also big festivals throughout the year, both religious and secular, and even with the chaos caused by the hundreds of thousands of migrants and the refugees from East Bengal, some remnants of ancient folkways, like the traveling dramatic shows which were a regular part of country life, still appear in Calcutta.

There are new types of theatre and literature, many with the popular theme of the clash between the old and the new, or East and West. Some of the well-to-do families still hold concerts of classical music or dance in their homes, rather than in a theatre or auditorium as is the Western concept. Certain Western plays have been adapted for the Bengali stage: I saw a magnificent performance of the Bertolt Brecht play, *The Threepenny Opera*, performed entirely in Bengali, with Bengali characters; since the Calcutta underworld is notorious, there was no great difficulty in making the transition from the colorful thieves of Restoration London to the recent past. And Chekov's *The Cherry Orchard* is performed regularly as a Bengali play, the decline of the landowner being as common a theme in Bengal as it was in nineteenth-century Russia. Of all the many peoples and races I have met in India, I

found the Bengalis the most interesting, charming and attractive. I had a number of conversations with Bengalis, and some of the flavor of their life and manner of thinking can be seen in these excerpts from what they told me.

india's most caustic critic is a small, wiry man, N.C. Chaudhuri. He has suffered greatly for his outspoken views. His two most famous works are *The Autobiography of an Unknown Indian*, an account of growing up in East Bengal and his life in Calcutta, and *The Continent of Circe*, which takes Indian history and character apart layer by layer, uncovering the tragic plight of his country with penetrating insight. One of his themes is that India is a nation of European warriors (the Aryans) who were emasculated by the frightful heat, the vast distances and the wars against the tribal aborigines.

When people come home from work, they come home to despair. The city is slowly sinking into the salt lakes. There is no hope for Calcutta unless half the population leaves the city and goes to work in the countryside. The bane of Calcutta has been the liking of Bengali intellectuals for sedentary desk jobs with a fixed salary. Tell a Bengali that you will give him a job measured in productivity: he will not take it. There is another factor: the lack of vitality. People who don't have energy must pay for safety. Does the tiger worry about his livelihood? In India, no one is rewarded for efficiency or punished for inefficiency. But no one wants to hear what I have to

Wandering street performers are common in the Indian cities. Here, a monkey man shows off his troupe for some school children.

say: such poverty, want and humiliation I have suffered for speaking the truth I cannot wish even an enemy.

Indian society has been security conscious in a very sordid way. Indians are not spiritual as you Westerners think. They are the most materialistic people on earth. The Indian languages — even Sanskrit — do not have a word for spirituality.

I am pessimistic, but there is some vitality in Calcutta. The young women have it, and no one else. I am the right age — in my seventies — and have a certain amount of renown, so I can talk to them. At first they are very shy. For an hour they say nothing, then that shyness disappears and their vitality comes to the surface. The hope for Calcutta is in the young women. Otherwise we will go down the drain.

Planning is our big escape. The experts make gigantic plans because nothing can be done. The plans are too big to get the money. They should start small: clean the streets, organize traffic. Elaborate plans do not mean accomplishment. We think that once we have the plans, the job is finished.

Everything has run down. The teaching of English, for example, is very bad. There is no cultural life in Calcutta. They'll tell you there is — you don't know the language and can't tell — but there is none.

The refugees are a big problem. They cause a lot of crime. Surround the refugee camps with police and give them a beating they won't forget for 500 years.

He talks as if he is trying to say everything at once. He is known all over India, and almost no one has a good word for him. "Oh, Chaudhuri!" people say, but I can tell that he has touched a raw nerve.

Bobby Bannerjee is a well-off business-man. Bengalis seem to like Western nicknames, like Dolly, Bunny, Baby, Sunny and so on. I never found out Bobby's Indian name. He has married an American girl, and hopes to immigrate to America some day. Indo-American marriages are not unusual among Bengalis of a certain high social and educational level, who are more open and independent than people from other provinces. The parents usually object, and the mother often exhibits psychosomatic illnesses that last for years if she thinks she is having any success in upsetting the young couple, but they usually are able to survive, and the half-dozen such marriages that I've encountered in Calcutta seem to be more than normally successful. Bannerjee likes to keep up a running monolog about Calcutta and Bengalis.

Calcutta is a huge garbage bin. Educated thieves are more in number than educated serfs. We get half-baked uneducated chaps as our ministers. I doubt that one of them has read more than five books in his entire life. Nobody has a thought for the other man. Every one of us would rather suffer than do anything anyone else might profit by. Friend of mine has a factory. Needs a road to get his products out, but he's refused to build it because other people would be able to use it. So they drag his products out along a trail full of garbage and excrement, and he's losing money because it's so inefficient.

I think a great deal can be done. We need a radical solution — not political — but one which breaks away from traditional modes of thinking. It's a question of money. Take

away the population pressures—people flock to Calcutta from Bihar, Orissa, Assam looking for work. The villages are empty. The population explosion is wrecking the plans for saving Calcutta. We should have good small villages with easy access to the city, with good roads, fast trains. Nobody, but nobody, realizes that Calcutta is taking half the population of West Bengal. The city was planned for a million, and even that was inadequate.

Sooner or later plans have to be made and they have to be carried out. Now we don't know where we are. We are faced with the facts of the Indian character. We are very secretive. No one will tell anyone else about his business, his life. How can we get the basic information to work with? Worse, people are unable to say Yes or No. It's built into the Indian character. Indecisiveness.

Have you ever tried to get a straight answer from an Indian?

Sabu Lal is a sweeper, which means that he spends his working day on his haunches cleaning floors. He is lucky enough to have a job with a large Western company, which means a better than usual salary. He lives, illicitly, in a corner of one of the company warehouses. The manager, an American, says, "I know he lives there. It's either that or

Sabu Lal, the sweeper, spends his working day on the floor.

The Kalighat, said by devotees of the goddess to be the most sacred spot in all India.

THE GANGES ∞ **156**

the street. He's got his wife, daughter and son with him too. Where the rest of our workers live, I don't know. I don't want to."

I came to Calcutta twenty years ago [says Sabu Lal to me]. My village is in Uttar Pradesh. Our farm is too small to support myself and my two brothers. There was not much we could do there, no place to go—we are untouchables—so one of my brothers and I came to Calcutta and left our other brother with the farm. Govind works in a paint factory here in Calcutta.

I earn 200 rupees a month. Either my wife or my daughter is in the village while the other one is here, so I send 150 home. It has been a good life here, working for the Americans [he smiles expansively]. I don't have a radio, but I go to the movies. Sometimes I go to the Kalighat to worship the goddess. I'd like to bathe in the river by the temple but the water is too dirty. [I ask him about re-incarnation.] I don't believe in all that nonsense. I won't be born again as a rich man. When I die I will go to heaven. But rebirth, no. If you are a good man, you will go to the place where God wants you to go.

I have trouble finding out his age. He eventually admitted to being forty-four. "To speak your age is to be it."

Mrs. Sarala Birla is a wife of a member of one of the three or four richest families in India. They own a great complex of factories and plants in both heavy and light industries—steel, air conditioners, bicycles, cottons, synthetics and so on. They also own a newspaper, *The Hindustani Times*, which is roughly the equivalent of *The New York Times*, and have offices and factories abroad in many countries, including Ethiopia, England, Scotland, Canada and the United States. The Birlas are from Rajasthan and are members of a caste devoted to business, the Mowraris, who are despised and envied by other Indians.

Controlling and reducing India's population is a necessity. The well-to-do people practice family planning, but the poor don't. You can see what will happen in fifty years if nothing is done—the World Health Organization estimates that India's population will be more than triple by then. We'll have a billion and a half people. The poor must be prevented from having so many children.

The Bengalis are lazy. It's the people from the other provinces like the Punjabis and the Sindis who work hard. The people must be made to work. The farmers have to work—they need new seeds and fertilizers and they must be made to use them. To do this India needs a dictator. [Of the Right or the Left, I ask.] Of the Right, of course.

Mrs. Birla shows me about their estate. It is a five-acre piece of land, known as Birla Park, and holds a large cluster of buildings, where the three Birla brothers live with their families. They had lived in a single house across the road, but it became too crowded, and now each family has its own house in the park, the earlier building being turned into a museum. The gardens are magnificently landscaped, with pools and little gazebos and antique statuary. The houses are large and airy, and the park is surrounded by a high wall, protected by strict guards who check each visitor. It is a hot day, and Mrs. Birla asks if I would like some almond juice. I say Yes, and when the bearer brings it in, toss if off quickly. She offers me another one, which I drink quickly, and then she tells me about the ice-skating rink, which is the only one in Calcutta and probably in all of India. Later I mention the almond juice to an American friend. "Almond juice!" says the American lady. "Nobody ever drinks almond juice like that. It costs about ten dollars a glass. And you had two!"

There is a narrow neck of land only thirteen miles wide between Bangladesh and Nepal leading into eastern India and the states of Assam and Meghalaya. Many of the people in this corridor are very primitive jungle tribals. In 1966 a group of tribals at a town called Naxalbari protested against the manner in which they were being exploited by one of the Indian landholders. The landholder shot at them, and the tribals attacked

The classical dance is perhaps India's most distinctive and creative, living artistic achievement. It is highly symbolic, expressing not only emotions but myth and the seasons through movement. This is a recital in Calcutta.

with farming tools and spears. A small war broke out, which was taken over by a pro-Maoist Indian Communist party. The revolt was crushed with a heavy loss of life among the tribals. Twelve hundred people were arrested, many of whom were held in prison without formal charges.

The incident at Naxalbari became the focus for a very radical anti-government movement, which earned the name of the Naxalites. The Naxalites were far more radical than the parent Communist parties from which they sprang, and were subsequently disowned by them. However, the Bengali character being volatile, independent, fiery, intelligent, the Naxalites eventually split into further groups, each claiming to be the authentic voice of the movement. At one time there were five Naxalite movements, according to one source, and perhaps more. Many of the Naxalites are students; others are industrial workers or farmers. Most of them are sincere and dedicated to the overthrow of the West Bengal government, and eventually the government of all of India. The industrial complex around Calcutta is infiltrated with Naxalites, and there are endless strikes and demonstrations, a constant undercurrent of violence. There have also been a number of assassinations and ordinary murders, for

The panchayat is the village council and is the central body of elders; it is called upon to settle disputes. Usually the panchayat is dominated by the highest caste in a village though other castes may have panchayats too.

which the Naxalites are blamed. On the other side, there is a great amount of repression from various sources. The formal Communist parties which have attained a certain amount of middle-class respectability have been trying to crush the Naxalites because they feel the movement is a danger to their own aims. And the government has just about abandoned normal democratic procedures in fighting the Naxalites. Anyone, particularly a student, who is suspected of being a Naxalite, is likely to be beaten or even killed by the police.

A Bengali businessman told me, quite sadly, that he had just returned from his ancestral village where he had seen the police work over some students. "The police broke off their arms and legs and left them to die in a ditch," he said, adding that he knew the boys and didn't think they were Naxalites. But people are using the movement to get rid of enemies or to pay off grudges. And the situation is complicated by dacoits holding up banks or shops and pretending to be Naxalites taking money to finance the movement's work. The Naxalites try to keep their identity a secret. I came to interview one through a roundabout method. He is an intelligent, intense young man, sickly (he has had tuberculosis). When I met him he lived with his parents in a middle-class "Communist" housing project outside Calcutta. His parents were confirmed Communists, but he grew up without interest in politics. Then, at the age of twenty, he found himself increasingly involved in left wing politics, and soon became more radical than his parents. "At first I had an intellectual assent to Communism," he said, "but now it has become a faith." He speaks English fluently, and was learning French, as well as translating *The Imitation of Christ* into Bengali, not from any religious convictions but because he needed the money. The missionary who gave him the job told me it was an excellent translation. He sits cross-legged on his charpoy, his eyes flashing, thoroughly convinced that he has taken the right step.

India's salvation [he tells me] will come only after bloodshed and chaos. We are opposed to American aid because it hoodwinks people from the main social problems. American aid is nothing but economic imperialism. It even affects Indian culture. Our basic problem is the domination of imperialistic capitalism and the survival of feudalism. The solution must be a Maoist one — to go back to the villages, build up a revolutionary base of a peoples' army which will consist largely of peasants and not so much of industrial workers. The villages will be

the fortresses of the revolution even when the general mass movement is at a low ebb. There can be no middle ground. The reactionary rightist forces will try to crush the peasants. The capitalists can't be indifferent because they will lose their markets. India will become another Vietnam.

America is the only effective power that can intervene to help the capitalists. It will be a protracted struggle, but the American people will support our policies. The time is ripe, conditions are mature. The peasants have suffered enough. They are ready for an armed insurrection. There is no democracy in India today. The task of the Communists in India is fundamentally to build up democracy. There is none for the peasants, the working people, the lower middle classes—only for a "miserable" minority. We have to establish a people's democracy, a dictatorship over landlords and capitalists. "All reactionaries are paper tigers," as Mao said. [I ask how the revolution will get weapons—from China?] That's a silly thing to propose. China can't afford to send weapons. The answer is that we will steal weapons from the enemy, that is, America. Your government will go all out to supply the Indian army. And then the revolutionaries will steal what they need. But weapons do not decide a war, people do. [And the devastion of such a revolution?] All the revolutions in the world, all the casualties, would be nothing compared to the annual deaths in India from malnutrition, famine and exploitation under capitalism . . . . In the final analysis we are bound to win. It may be after my death, after decades, after centuries, but we will win. It's no dream, it's inevitable. It's independent of my will, your will. It's inexorable, inevitable.

His eyes flash and he stares straight into my face. The next time I was in Calcutta I asked my contact if I could see the boy. "Not a chance," I am told. "He's hiding in the jungle. He's training in the Naxalite forces."

Demonstrations are a common sight in Calcutta. Here a group of peasants have come from outlying villages to hold a protest meeting on the city's great maidan or park.

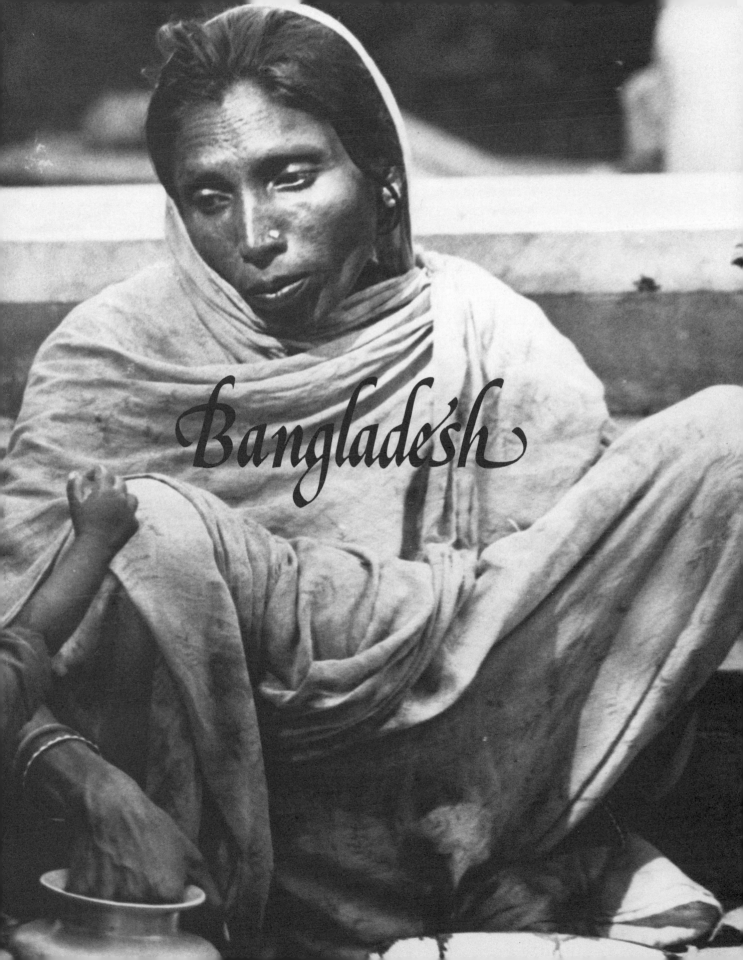

Deep in East Bengal the Ganges is joined by the Brahmaputra, which has come down from Tibet through Assam. Both rivers break up into several slow-moving, muddy branches, which meander through the vast delta. During the day the sky is white-hot, not turning to a color until the late afternoon, when the sun becomes vivid orange and drops like a flaming ball into streaks of violently pink and red clouds behind the gray sky. In the misty mornings the endless riverscape is lost in the haze; this is the time when people go into the fields and rivers and ponds to defecate and then to wash. The network of rivers and canals is complex; they flow between banks of sand and mud, reeds and water hyacinth. The water is tidal and slightly brackish, but there are fresh water porpoises leaping and splashing in magnificent arches. The women wash their clothes along the shores; on the banks the children tend the cattle. Heron, egrets, water buffalo stand silently in the reeds. The river traffic is endless: slim fishing boats with high sweeping prows and sterns like black crescent moons, swift cargo boats with big square patched sails, steam boats and motor launches. In the canals off the rivers are colonies of water gypsies.

The rivers are the thoroughfares and the source of life. While most of the great land mass of India and West Pakistan is barren and dry, the delta is rich with water. The people of the delta live on, in and by water. Water is life for them, but it is also death, because, even more than in Calcutta, the delta is rife

with cholera, so much so that the nations of SEATO, the South-East Asian Treaty Organization (of which the United States is a member) selected the East Bengal delta for a comprehensive study of cholera in the hopes that a cure could be found somewhere in those turgid waters. The Bengal delta is the one area in the world where cholera is endemic; it is present on a year-round basis, instead of sporadically as in most other affected areas. Cholera peaks twice in the delta, and thousands of people die.

But cholera is not the only affliction. East Bengal, and the adjoining Indian coast, are especially prone to hurricanes and cyclones. Periodically, great storms have devastated the coastal areas. In 1876 a storm swept East Bengal, killing 300,000 people and leveling whole villages. In the past fifty years alone, forty-two cyclones have come to the same areas. But the greatest tragedy of all was the cyclone of November 12, 1970, which was the worst in known history. In the center of a cyclone is a whirling wind, which can reach speeds of 200 miles an hour; this is called the eyewall, and the eyewall of November 12th pushed a jagged wall of water before it, estimated by some of the survivors as being sixty feet high.

The cyclone had been spotted by an American weather satellite and vague warnings were sent out by the govern-

A young girl draws water in a Hindu village in Bangladesh. Most of the Hindu population of East Bengal was killed during the war of 1971.

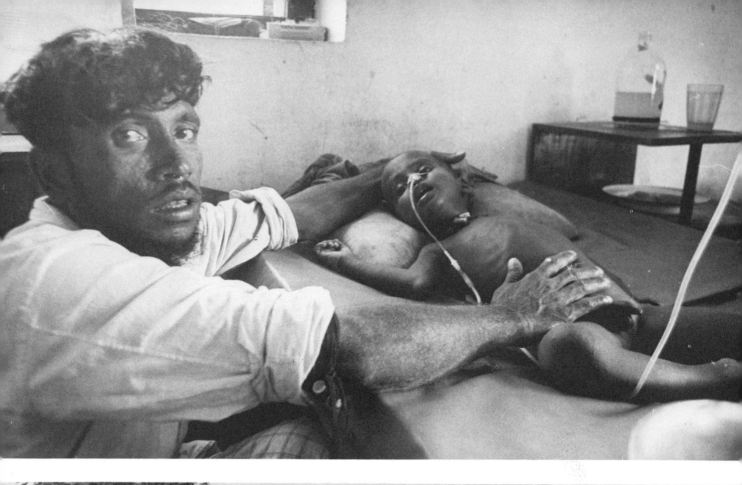
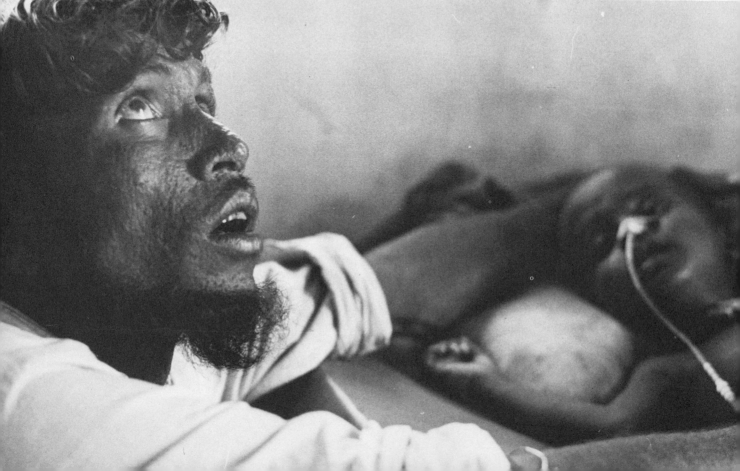

ment in Dacca, the capital of what was then East Pakistan. But not many of the people received the warning, and even if they had, there was no place in which to hide. There is no flood control system, the land is rarely higher than twenty feet, and the best one can do is to climb a tree or to the roof of a house. Since it is a land of waterways and not roads, it was not easy to get away from the area. When the eyewall hit, swelling into a deafening roar, everything vanished beneath it. A blinding wind swept over the wreckage. The survivors of its first onrush now found the eyewall coming back in a huge, muddy, choking, debris-ridden flood. By the time the eyewall had finally subsided, there was very little life left in the fifty-mile path it had cut. Communications were destroyed, and it was two days before Dacca realized that the damage had been crippling. Because there is no census of East Bengal there is no calculating the number of people killed or lost, but all the crops, which were ready for the harvest, were destroyed. Severe famine followed, along with cholera and other plagues caused by the unsanitary conditions resulting from tens of thousands of unburied dead—people and animals. Reporters who visited the area in the following weeks said the survivors were in a state of shock: numb and expressionless.

At a cholera clinic on a branch of the Ganges in Bangladesh a father cares for his son. The boy is getting a saline treatment; if aid is given as soon as the patient falls ill, cholera can usually be cured.

East Bengal is one of the most beautiful places I have ever seen. The endless waterways, from the broad rivers to the tiny canals and tributaries, give it a deeply poetic appearance. Yet life there is unbearably hard. Foreign financial experts compute the per capita income at $30 a year, but, says an American reporter who was there during the beginning of the 1971 war, this figure is so low "that many economists refuse to believe it, arbitrarily raising it to $50 on the grounds that there must be some mistake in available data." Only fifteen percent of the inhabitants are believed to be literate. Yet, in the villages I visited the people were exceptionally neat and clean. I entered houses in a Muslim village where all possessions were neatly hanging from walls or rafters, and the floors, which were of mud, were, as Americans like to say, "clean enough to eat off of," which in the case of the Indian and Pakistani peasant is not a metaphor but a fact. Normally one sits on the floor and food is served on a fresh green banana frond.

There are few natural resources, such as minerals. Revenue is derived from tea, tobacco, timber, fish, and normally jute, but the mills are on the Indian side of the border. Rice and wheat, which are staples of the diet, must normally be imported, and with the two great cyclones and the civil war, imports are at a minimum.

It is late November and the cholera season is peaking, with cases beginning to pile up in the hospitals. A report in the English-language newspaper in Dacca says that in the previous six weeks 1,500 cases were reported, with 425 deaths in a locality a few miles north of Dacca. There was only one medical team at work there, consisting of students serving on an around-the-clock basis. In an area as large as New York State and Connecticut combined, there are only two hospitals for cholera cases, one in Dacca, and the other about forty miles south in a landing called Matlab Bazar. At the time of the cholera season both were filled to overflowing. The press had daily reports on the spread of the epidemic and attacked the authorities for being impassive, as they usually are. The major cause of the quick spread of illness was the lack of pure water in the villages and in Dacca itself. One newspaper charged that "Overhead tanks from which water is being supplied are not properly cleaned." Pipes leak and "bacteria and worms enter smoothly." And, "At present the duration of water supply varies from twelve hours to seventeen hours," a common complaint everywhere in the subcontinent. Public authorities had suggested that water be boiled, but in a country with such endemic poverty, the money to buy extra wood for boiling water did not exist, and thus the epidemic spread. The doctor in charge of the SEATO cholera research laboratory, reported, "Our epidemiologists estimate that in East Pakistan with a population of over 60,000,000 there are probably over 100,000 cases per annum." The interesting thing about cholera, which is a disease that is borne almost completely through water and affects only man, is that if it is treated in the first few hours, the victim's chance of survival is almost 100 percent. Medication is simple, requiring primarily the replacement of liquids and salts in large quantities. But if he is not treated the patient's chance of death runs as high as sixty percent.

Ahead of us, the porpoises break in great arcs. The jungle overwhelms. Massive banyan trees lean precariously over the banks where the snowy egrets hunt for frogs amid the hyacinth and water lilies. We leave the main river and go through a silent canal, sometimes so narrow the grass on the banks touches our boat. Then it broadens and is spanned by a delicate soaring bridge of bamboo, its struts as fine as a spider's web. Three slim women, carrying clay pitchers on their heads, stop briefly to watch. Coming around a sharp bend we surprise a colony of water gypsies probing the river bottom with spears. Some children run along the bank and then stop in wonder: such a pale face this one man has! It is an idyllic landscape, and I fall in love with it—with its lushness, its rich greens which run from emerald in the paddy fields to a deeper tint in the jute, to olive and black in the forests; and with the people, so graceful, charming and animated. Then we turn into another wide river. The sun is beginning to set, and I ask the boatman to stop so I can watch it in peace. Now it is becoming

A young boy washes himself in the town tank after a meal. The same water is used for bathing, drinking, and laundry.

dark. I meet some friends at a river landing; they have a jeep and we speed through the dusk because we have to catch a ferry before it stops running for the night. Suddenly the front right wheel begins to bump. We have a flat, but Ali, the driver, jumps out, jacks up the car, and fixes the tire in a few minutes. We reach the ferry just as the crew is about to pull in the gangplank. The sun has gone, and now the moon is rising, luminous, ancient, Indian. The ferry is a small, open raft with a small bridge; it stinks of oil. The pilot has a transistor radio which is playing at full volume, as do all radios in Pakistan and India. "Army music," says Ali scornfully. The government, which controls the radio station, is playing Urdu songs over the Bengali radio. "That is what they think of us," says one of my friends. "We are a colony for the Punjabis." Everyone looks around nervously to see if there might be any Punjabis, that is, West Pakistanis, present, and then the storm breaks loose, the sad story of West Pakistan's exploitation of East Bengal. Here is the natural wealth, here is the bulk of Pakistan's population, here is culture and intelligence, and East Bengal is nothing but a colony for the Twenty-Two Families of the West and their military government. "We are going to explode," says Ali. "Soon."

The cyclone subsided; the uncounted dead, the lost, the maimed and the ill were mourned. The land deceptively appeared recovered. New growth burgeoned wildly. But an even greater tragedy was to strike East Bengal. In December, 1970, a few weeks after the great cyclone had passed, Pakistan held elections for the National Assembly. This was the first time since its founding in 1947 that candidates for the nation's Assembly were to be freely chosen. The issues involved reflected the division of Pakistan into two units. In the West, the candidates more or less supported a strong central government which would continue the military dictatorship. In the East, the Bengali candidates, mostly members of the Awami League—a movement that sought some kind of regime autonomy—proposed a six-point program which would leave certain governmental affairs, such as foreign relations, in the hands of the West, but would allow East Bengal control over its resources, industry, and civil administration, and would share taxes fairly and keep East Bengal earnings at home instead of letting the businessmen of the West drain them off. The Awami League was founded by a brooding, selfless man named Sheik Mujibir Rahman. Since East Bengal has two thirds of the population, the Awami League gained the majority of the seats in the new Assembly, and Mujib, as he was popularly known, was obviously to become a major figure in the government. But the West was not to allow this show of Bengali independence.

Four days before the Assembly was to meet in the capital at Islamabad in West Pakistan, the Pakistani President Yahya Khan announced its postponement. Meanwhile troops from the West were secretly sent by ship around India and moved into Bengal. The East Bengalis were furious with the postponement. Demonstrations and protest meetings erupted spontaneously, and Mujib announced a province-wide, five-day general strike, which effectively closed down every factory, office, shop, school, government office, and all transportation, even bicycles. Yahya Khan sent as administrator of East Bengal a tough Punjabi general, Tikka Khan, popularly known as the Butcher of Baluchistan because of his ruthlessness in putting down a revolt among the fierce tribes along Pakistan's border with Iran. It was obvious that Tikka Khan's mission was not to serve as a mediator. The Chief Justice of the Dacca High Court refused to swear him in as governor. Events seemed to be rushing beyond anyone's control. Yahya Khan himself came to Dacca to confer with Sheik Mujibir. Each man, in his public statements, charged that the other refused to negotiate or compromise.

On the evening of March 25, Yahya Khan boarded his plane to fly back to Karachi, no progress having been made in his talks with the East Bengalis. A few hours later his troops, virtually all from the West, struck without warning, attacking Dacca as if it were an enemy city, with tanks, mortars and machine guns. Dacca was unprepared. The Army swept through the streets with the violence of the Turks and Moghuls in an orgy of killing and destruction. Sheik Mujibir had asked his people to practice non-violence, but he warned them that bloodshed was virtually inevitable. He had also warned them that they must be prepared for the "ultimate sacrifice," and that he himself might not be alive to lead them. Early in the morning of the 26th the Army arrested the Sheik, and for weeks he was believed dead, until rumors appeared saying he was being held in a prison in the West. "Why can't they let us part as brothers?" he had asked in one of his last public speeches. "I am a man of peace and non-violence. If it comes to bloodshed and war, others will take over, more radical—very possibly the Communists—and there will be another Vietnam."

The Army swept through East Bengali, arresting or shooting down Bengalis of all types, government officials, intellectuals, teachers, businessmen. Army officers from Bengal were seized and executed without any pretense at trial or a hearing; the Bengali soldiers were arrested and imprisoned, and then many of them were shot by the Punjabis. Riots and protests brought further reprisals. The Punjabis raided villages, shooting down the men and raping the women. There was some sporadic resistance, particularly from Bengalis who had been in the Army, and from police who had access to arms. Meanwhile, people began to flee into India, which surrounds East Bengal on all its land borders. First there were hundreds, then they came by the hundreds of thousands, and then by the million. The resistance movement seemed to die out and then it appeared that it was holding on. A new, independent government was formed in the small pieces of territory held by the resisters. It was called Bangladesh, the Land of the Bengalis, and the rebel forces were known as Mukti Bahini, the Freedom Brotherhood. Western reporters who went to the refugee camps heard the same story over and over again—the Punjabis were raiding villages, shooting and looting indiscriminately, burning houses and crops, and raping the girls. "It is going to be hell for us," said Mrs. Indira Gandhi, India's Prime Minister, as the refugees first began to flood her country. But India set up camps, found food, even though her own people live on the starvation level, and counted somewhere between nine and ten million refugees within her borders in the first eight months. It was costing India a million dollars a day to care for them. Meanwhile the slaughter in East Bengal continued.

By the time the question of Bangladesh was brought up in the United Nations in early December of the same year, it was commonly believed that a million people had been killed by the West Pakistani armed forces, a figure that was never challenged but merely explained by Yahya Khan as necessary for restoring "peace" in Bengal. Mrs. Gandhi made a hurried trip to the Western world, to America and Europe, to ask for help, but was unsuccessful. The Mukti Bahini grew stronger, receiving weapons from India. Pakistani troops were reported firing into India, and Indian troops made forays into East Bengal. The war was escalating. Shortly after Mrs. Gandhi had left the White House in a bitter mood because she had been unable to get aid for the refugees, the President announced that America was cutting off its foreign aid to India for her violation of Pakistani territory. West Pakistan bombed cities and airfields in western India, and Indian troops joined the Mukti Bahini in active collaboration, forcing the surrender of the Punjabi troops, who were now outnumbered. A new Pakistani ambassador to America arrived at the White House with his charming wife and even more charming daughter, where he was, according to the American press "warmly received." The President said: "We have followed with sympathetic interest the efforts of the Government and people of Pakistan to achieve an amicable political settlement in East Pakistan. We have also welcomed the efforts of President Yahya to move to reduce tensions in the subcontinent." The next night the General Assembly of the United Nations voted 104 to 11 (with ten abstentions) for a resolution urging India and Pakistan to stop fighting and to pull back their troops. Both nations ignored the resolution. A million dead Bengalis and 10,000,000 refugees were the toll of the tragedy. The morning after the vote, the White House, as it had been saying all week, repeated that "India was the aggressor in the war."

In a remote village in Bangladesh a group of children gather around the photographer, the first foreigner they have ever seen. Some are frightened, others curious. "Such pale skin this man has!" they say.

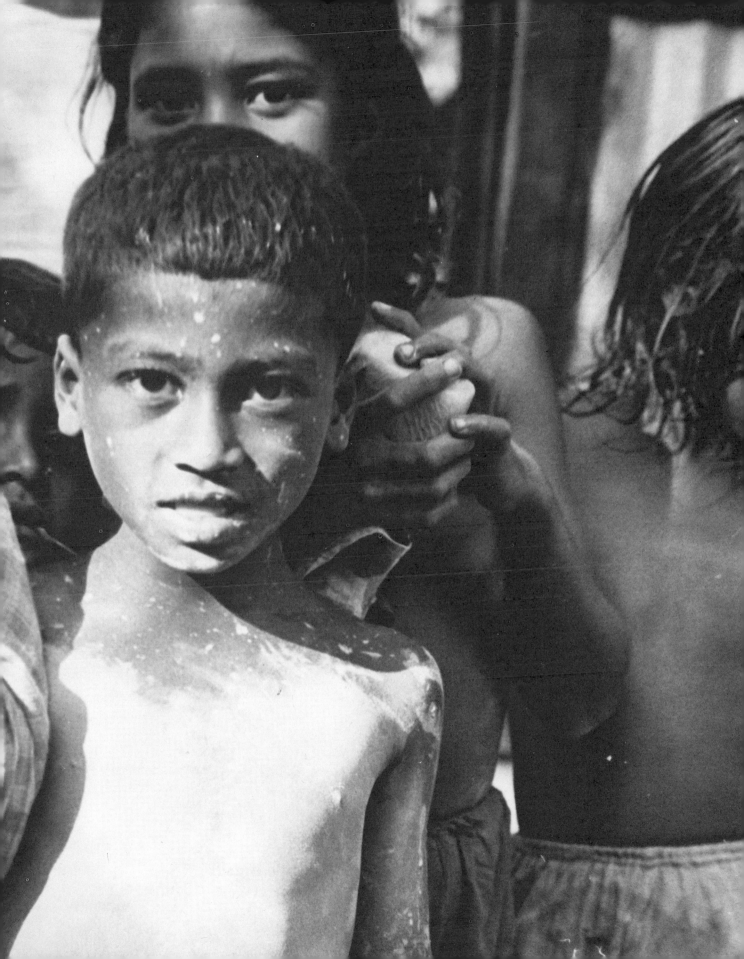

Benares. It is a steaming hot morning. I have been looking for an Indian professor who teaches philosophy at Benares Hindu University. He lives at Hanuman Ghat (named after the monkey god), and with the aid of an old man who seems to have nothing to do except bring strangers to the professor's house, I am led through a series of narrow alleys, virtually blocked by sacred cows, to the top of the ghat. The view is magnificent. Far below I can see some Muslim washermen, the dobhis, flailing their laundry against huge stones, and across the Ganges is the flat plain that leads imperceptibly into the white-hot sky. The professor has a tiny, two-story house, next to a temple. I bang on the door, and finally it opens and a Western woman—she is French—looks out cautiously. I ask for the professor. "He is away," she says, peevishly. She doesn't know when he will return, perhaps in a week, perhaps not. The woman is wearing a sari and is barefoot. I try to get some information out of her, but it is difficult. She has changed her name to Shanti, which means peace in Hindi, and hopes to become an Indian citizen. "I suppose you're going back to America and write a book about India," she said. I wasn't—then—but said Yes to test her reaction. "You ought to know better," she said, "it takes ten years to understand the Indian mind." Later I repeated the conversation to an Indian woman in Bombay. She laughed and said, "Well, it takes *twenty* to understand the Western mind."

The Ganges delta. It is dusk. The dying reflection of the sun is caught in the silent waters of the swamps, flickering among the lilies and the lotuses. A boat glides by, poled by a small boy anxious to return home before the blackness overwhelms him. The night sounds emerge: frogs and insects, birds, a dog barking, someone playing a small flute, a transistor radio rasping movie music. The air is sweet with the scent of mogras and lilac, of the tropic earth. The Hundred Mouths of Ma Ganga are now black in the heavy night. Throughout the delta are the buried secrets of cyclone, famine, rebellion and war. The jungle and the rivers are swallowing the traces of a ravaged land, the victims of the storms, the villagers murdered by the Punjabis, the cholera dead, the West Pakistanis ambushed by the Mukti Bahini, the invading Indian jawans.

The refugees have long since returned to their villages, squatting on their haunches amid the ruins of their villages: houses gutted, crops lost, memories of executions and rapes flooding their minds. The months in the Indian refugee camps fade away as the hamlets and villages and towns are reconstructed. But this green, unhappy land is to have no rest: famine and hunger follow; cholera strikes again. Each succeeding year seems to bring no relief from the problems. Bengalis who once fought the Pakistanis now find enemies among their Bengali brothers. The Sheik, half blind since youth, tries to hold on—he is the only leader the people can follow—

but meanwhile there are new rebels in the jungles, in the Dacca slums, in the student cafes, in the mills. Food prices rise, and the rice crop fails. Jute, the great cash crop upon which the nation is so dependent, falls by forty percent. India, which had been so generous to the refugees and had risked an international war by aiding the Bengalis (for American warships had threatened the Bay of Bengal), is now called the "enemy" by some of the extremists.

On the southern shore of Sagar Island, the last piece of Bengal before the open waters of the Bay, where parents once sacrificed their children to Mother Ganges in honor of her liberation of the raja's burnt sons, the devout now worship a block of stone that represents Kapila, the crusty sage whose fiery body sent the princes to the depths of hell. Today the pilgrims throw small, worthless gems into the ocean from the beach. Fifteen hundred miles away and three miles higher, Ma Ganga splashes onto Shiva's matted hair, cool and clear with the joy of a river just come down from heaven. All across the great plain of Hindustan, Mother Ganges gathers up fragments of her India, the ashes of her people, the soil of her farms, watering and nourishing, creating and destroying and recreating, flowing silently, olive black, limpid, mysterious, eternal. Slowly Mother Ganges is absorbed into the Bay of Bengal, watering the shores of Burma, Thailand, southeast Asia, the world.

The Celestial Ganga

King Yudhisthira, sage, Ruler of the World, who has seen his brothers the Pandavas and his cousins the Kauravas destroy each other in war and its aftermath, at last dies and is about to enter the celestial heaven.

Indra, warrior, god of all gods, dancer, magician, aspect of Shiva, calls:

O mighty Yudhisthira! Join the ranks of the celestials who are pleased with you. Illusions have ended. Let the fever of your heart be dispelled. Here is the celestial river, sacred and sanctifying the three worlds. It is called the celestial Ganga. Plunging into it, you will attain your proper place.

And Yudhisthira [according to the Mahabharata]:

Having bathed in the celestial river Ganga sacred and purifying,
he renounced his human body.
Assuming a celestial form
Yudhisthira the Just, through that bath became divested of all hatreds and sorrows.
Surrounded by the celestials
he finally reached the place
where those heroes, his kinsmen,
were enjoying
each his respective
position.

iNDEX

East India Company, 41, 86,
87, 88, 94, 126, 134
opium trade, 126–127
Sepoy Mutiny, 94, 97,
98–101, 103, 104, 105,
144
Enquiry into India, An, 60
Epics. *See* Literature, sacred;
Vedas
Eternal Mother
cows as symbols of, 33
Ethiopia, 158
Everest, Mount, 12

Fable
origin of opium, 127
Family, extended, 38
Famine, 38, 41, 143, 163, 169,
176
Farming, 18, 21. *See also*
Agriculture
Fertilizer, 124
Final Solution, 115
Five Rivers, 12
Flooding, 2, 3, 16, 23, 38, 39,
45, 123, 140, 142, 167, 169
Flora Domestica, 127
Florence
Hardwar as the Indian, 32
Food, 27, 95, 100, 121
Food for Work program, 124
Foreign aid
to Pakistan and India, 147
Foreign relief, 120, 122, 135,
136
Forrest, Sir George W., 105
Forster, E. M., 69
Fragmentation
of farming land, 21

Freedom Brotherhood, 173

Gandharan, 56
Gandhi, Indira, 152, 173, 174
Gandhi, Mahatma, 150
Gangadwar, 30
Ganga, Princess, 4
Gangastottara-sata-hamvali, 9
Ganges
Canal, 31–32, 38, 41
purity of water, 115–116, 118
sacred names, 9
source, 2, 4–6, 26
three forms, 108
tributaries, 12, 13
Ganges plain. *See* Gangetic
plain
Gangetic plain, 15, 16, 17–18,
19, 37, 45, 46, 51, 52, 56, 58,
61, 67, 87, 130
Gangotri Glacier, 4
Ganja, 111
Garhwal Himalayas, 4
Garuda, 5
Gaznivids, 60, 61
Genghis Khan, 65
Geography
of India, 12–23
Geology
Himalayas, 17
India, 12–13
Ghats, 113, 150, 157, 176
Ghazipur, 38
Ghazni, Mahmud of, 60
Ghee, 5, 122
Goa, 86
Gods, 31, 45, 68, 136. *See also*
Kali; Krishna; Shiva
Goethe, 130

Golden Paradise, 53
Gondwara, 12
Govind, 111
Grant, Charles, 88
Great Goddess, 45
Greeks, 44, 45, 46, 56, 58. *See
also* Alexander the Great
language, 49
Gunas, 9
Guptas, 129–134
Gypsies, water, 166, 170

Haldia, 141–142
Hanuman Ghat, 176
Harappa, 44–45, 46
Hardwar, 27, 30, 31–36, 38
Har Ki Pairi, 31, 33
Hash, 113
Hastinapura, 52–53
Hastings, Warren, 87, 90
Heaven
descent of Ganges from,
4–6, 177
Herelle, Dr. D., 116
Herodotus, 56
Himalayas, 2, 4, 12, 13, 17, 45,
134
Hindi, 136, 137, 176
Hinduism, 2, 3, 4–6, 12, 33, 46,
56, 59, 60, 68, 93, 94,
108–109, 121–122
ancient cosmology of, 3, 45,
59
elements of, in Indus valley
civilization, 45
Hindu Kush, 57
Hindustan, 65, 177
Hindustani Times, The, 158

O

Old Delta
  at Bengal, 140, 141
OM, 33
Opium, 111
  trade, 126–127, 134–135
Opium Godown, 126
Orissa, 87, 142, 151, 155
Oude, 100. *See also* Oudh
Oudh
  king of, 99
  and Sepoy Mutiny, 99–101
Overpopulation, 13, 158. *See
  also* Population
Oxen, 123

P

Pacific islands, 18
Paddy, 20, 170
Pahlavas, 58
Painted Gray Ware, 52
Painting, 63, 95, 130
Pakistan, 12, 15, 18, 41, 69,
  95, 145, 147, 158, 171, 174.
  See also East Pakistan; West
  Pakistan
Pali, 46
Panchkosi Road, 109
Pandavas, 179
Pandit, 36
Pandu brothers, 67
Pangaea, 12
"Paper tigers," 163
Parthians, 58
Parliament, English, 87, 99
Partition of 1947, 69
  refugees after, 147
Passage to India, A, 69

Patala Ganges, 108
Pataliputra, 53, 57, 128
Patna, 56, 67, 126, 128
Persia, 56, 64
  language, 49
Phallic worship, 45
Philippines, 18, 59
Pilgrims, 26, 30, 31, 108, 177
Pingala, 108
Plagues, 15. *See also* Disease
Plain
  Ganges. *See* Gangetic plain
  Indus, 19
Plassey, "battle" of, 87
Plateau, Chota Nagpur, 141
Poe, Edgar Allen, 127
Politics
  modern, in India, 69
Poppy plant. *See* Opium
Poppy-seed Lady, 127
Population
  Benares, 112, 115
  Calcutta, 142, 151, 156
  East Pakistan, 170
  Muslim, of Bengal, 144
  over-, 13, 158
Portuguese, 86, 95
Pottery, 45, 46, 52
Poverty, 33, 38, 151, 152
Prayag, 31
"Prohibited area," 27
Public buildings
  British, 95
  Muslim, 64
Pulses, 121
Punjab, 12, 41, 57, 60, 104, 158
Punjabis, 151, 171, 176. *See
  also* West Pakistan
Purity
  of Ganges' water, 115–116,
  118

Putari, 124
Pyre, funeral, 91. *See also Sati*

Q

Question of Milander, 56

R

Rabi, 23
Rahman, Sheik Mujibir, 172,
  173, 176
Rainfall, 19, 20. *See also*
  Monsoon
Rajas, 9, 92
Rajastan, 151, 158
Rajmahal, 39
Ramparts
  Mohenjo-daro–Harappa, 46
Rawalpindi-Islamabad, 145
Refugees
  from East Bengal, 151, 153,
    155, 173, 176, 177
  Hindu, after Partition, 141
Regulating Act of 1784, 87
Reincarnation, 157
"Releaser of the three debts," 9
Religion
  Aryan, 45
  Buddhism, 58, 59, 129
  Christianity, 59, 88, 90
  Hinduism, 45, 59, 60
  Islam, 71, 144, 145
Revolutionaries, 133, 150, 161
Rice, 20, 23, 52, 123, 124, 142,
  144
Rickshawallahs, 111
Rig-Veda, 46
Rishikesh, 26, 27, 32
Rishis, 26, 30, 127
Rites, 5, 112

sati, 91, 93–94
Roman empire, 130
Roman numerals, 59, 60
Romantics, European, 130

S

Sacred cow, 33, 100, 150
Sacred nectar, 31
Sacred waters
    of goddess Ganga, 5
Sacred writings. *See* Literature,
    sacred
Sacrifice, child, 88, 91, 94,
    177
Sadhus, 27, 30, 35
Sagar, 4, 5
Sagar Island, 31, 91, 177
Saharanpur, 39
Sakas, 58
Sakuntala, 130
Sandracottus, Emperor, 128
Sannyasis, 27
Sanskrit, 3, 6, 46, 56, 130, 154
Sarasvati, 12, 30
Sari, 95, 109, 110, 111
Sarnath, 111
Sasaram, 125
Sati (goddess), 93
Sati (rite), 91, 93–94
Sattva, 9
Script, Devanagari, 57
Scriptures, Hindu, 4, 51. *See*
    also Literature, sacred
SEATO, 167, 169
Secret police
    of Chandragupta, 129
Sects, 28, 35. *See also*
    Shaivites; Vaishnuvites
Separatist movement
    East Pakistan, 69, 144–145

Sepoy, 100. *See also* Sepoy
    Mutiny
Sepoy Mutiny, 94, 97, 98–101,
    103, 104, 105, 144
Seven Sacred Cities, 27
Seven Sacred Rivers, *xi*
Shah, Bahadur, 100, 101
Shaivites, 6, 27
Shiva, Lord, 2, 6, 16, 30, 33, 45,
    59, 93, 108, 177, 179
Shrines, 51, 68
Sikhs, 35, 41, 103, 104
Silting, 18, 38, 39, 41, 142
Sind, 44, 45, 158
Sites, archeological, 44–45,
    51–52
Sivananda, Swami, 116
Slavery, 88, 90
Sleeman, Sir William, 91
Social class. *See* Caste
Solnai, 41
Son, 12, 121, 125, 136
"Soul substance," *xiii*
Source
    of Ganges, 2, 4–6
South Asia, 12
Southeast Asia, 18, 59, 177
South-East Asian Treaty
    Organization, 167, 169
South India, 86
South Pacific, 59
Spencer, Major, 103
Steel industry, 41
Sugar cane, 142
Sumati, 4
Surs, 31
Sushumna, 108
Suttee, 91. *See also* Sati
Swamis, 27
Symbol
    of Eternal Mother, 33

of Lord Shiva, 33, 108
phallic, 33

T

Taboos, food, 27, 100
Taj Mahal, 68
Tamas, 9
Tapovan, 30
Taxes, 133, 134
Taxila, king of, 56
Tea
    Bangladesh and Assam and,
        142
    China trade for, 126
Tectonic trough, 17–18
Temples, 16, 38, 57, 59, 60, 108
Thailand, 59, 177
Thar Desert, 19
Theology, Muslim, 68
Third World, 126
Threepenny Opera, The, 153
Thucydides, 46
Tibet, 12, 13, 17, 26, 45, 166
Timur, 64, 65
Tobacco, 23, 95, 142
Topis, 95
Trade, 12, 52, 56, 130, 134
    East India Company and, 41,
        86, 87, 88, 94, 126
    opium, 126–127, 134–135
Trading posts, 39, 86
Transportation, 36, 45, 56, 95,
    109, 111, 134, 135, 142, 166
Tribal peoples, 44, 51–52, 58
    present day. *See* Tribals
Tribals, 158
Tributaries
    of the Ganges, 12, 13, 38
Trident
    of Shiva, 33, 108

Tuberculosis, 161
Tughlaq, 63, 65
Turco-Persian rulers, 37
Turkestan, Chinese, 58
Turks, 37, 60, 61, 64, 65
Twenty-Two Families
   of West Pakistan, 145, 171
Two Rivers, 13

Ujjain, 31
Ujjala theatre, 150
Underworld Ganges, 108
United Nations, 173, 174
United Province, 39
Universal Being, 3, 59
University, Benares Hindu, 176
Untouchables, 157
Upanishads, 46, 49
Upper Doab, 52
Urban development, 112
Urdu, 145, 171
Uttar Pradesh, 38, 110, 141,
   142, 151, 157

Vaishnavites, 6, 27
Valley, Damodar, 141

Varanesi, 108
Vedas, 28, 46
Vedic scriptures, 9
Vegetarians, 27
Village life, early, 37–38
Vishnu, Lord, 6, 24
Voyage to East Indies, A, 116

Warfare, 53, 60, 69, 128, 129.
   See also Domination, foreign
   British conquest, 87, 94
   Civil War in East Bengal,
      172–174
   Opium War, 126
   Sepoy Mutiny, 94, 99–101,
      103
Water, 3–4, 38, 115–116, 118,
   166, 170
Water buffalo, 166
Well-digging, 123–124
Wellesley, Richard, 87
Wellington, Arthur Wellesley,
   Duke of, 87
West, the, 13, 45, 46, 49, 56,
   130
   Indian influence on, 59–60
West Bengal, 140, 141, 147, 161
Westernization

of Indians, 95
West Pakistan, 15, 44, 145. *See
   also* Pakistan; Punjabis
   Civil War in, 171–174
   Twenty-Two Families of, 171
Wheat, 20, 124
Wheel, Persian, 123
Widows, 125. *See also Sati*
World Health Organization, 158
World War II, 69, 143
Wren, Christopher, 95
Writing, sacred. *See* Literature,
   sacred
Wu-san, 58

Xerxes, 56

Yensisey, 2
Yorktown
   battle of, 87
Yudhisthira, 179
Yueh-chi, 58

Zero, 59–60